Augustine's Relic

Augustine's Relic

Lessons from the Oldest Book in England

KIRK SMITH

Morehouse Publishing
NEW YORK

Unless otherwise noted, the Scripture quotations contained herein are from the New Revised Standard Version Bible, copyright © 1989 by the Division of Christian Education of the National Council of Churches of Christ in the U.S.A. Used by permission. All rights reserved.

Morehouse Publishing, 19 East 34th Street, New York, NY 10016

Morehouse Publishing is an imprint of Church Publishing Incorporated.
www.churchpublishing.org

Cover design by Jennifer Kopec, 2Pug Design
Typeset by PerfecType, Nashville, Tennessee

Library of Congress Cataloging-in-Publication Data
Names: Smith, Kirk, 1951- author.
Title: Augustine's relic : lessons from the oldest book in England / Kirk Smith.
Description: New York, NY : Morehouse Publishing, 2016.
Identifiers: LCCN 2015037022 | ISBN 9780819232267 (pbk.) | ISBN 9780819232274 (ebook)
Subjects: LCSH: St. Augustine Gospels. | Bible. Gospels–Manuscripts. | Manuscripts, Latin (Medieval and modern)–England. | Books–England--History–400-1450. | England–Church history. | Mission of the church. | Mass media–Religious aspects–Anglican Communion. | Internet in church work. | Anglican Communion–Relations–Catholic Church. | Catholic Church–Relations–Anglican Communion. | Augustine, Saint, Archbishop of Canterbury, -604? | Parker, Matthew, 1504-1575.
Classification: LCC BS2552.S75 S55 2016 | DDC 226/.047–dc23 LC record available at http://lccn.loc.gov/2015037022

Printed in the United States of America

A.D. 596: Her Gregorius papa sende to Brytene Augustinum. mid wel manegum munecum. þe Godes word Engla ðeoda godspelledon.

596 CE: This year Pope Gregory sent Augustine to Britain with very many monks, to preach the word of God to the English people.

—*Anglo-Saxon Chronicle*

Contents

Preface

I have always loved old books. When I was a child visiting my grandparents, I would pore over old notebooks and photographs that had once belonged to my ancestors. Bookstores, especially those stocked with rare dusty volumes, became my favorite haunts when I was in high school and college. As an undergraduate visiting England, one of my most lasting memories was a journey to the British Library (then in its old location at the British Museum), where I was able to press my nose close to glass cases containing such treasures as the Codex Sinaiticus, the Lindisfarne Gospels, and Magna Carta, not to mention works by J. S. Bach and James Joyce.

To me such books and manuscripts were more than simply relics of the past, they were almost mystical portals into the lives of those men and women I had learned about in history class, icons of a strange and vanished world. Fans of the BBC science fiction series *Doctor Who* will understand what I mean when I say that for me an old book became a kind of a TARDIS to another point in time and space!

When I became a graduate student in medieval history, my favorite courses were those on paleography, the study of ancient writing. Deciphering the text of medieval documents with their complex systems of abbreviations and detecting the date and provenance of a manuscript based upon the scribe's particular style of writing was always an exciting and engaging challenge.

But even as a novice historian I was also aware that such manuscripts were more than simply intriguing puzzles; they were in fact important tools in understanding the larger culture that produced them. Every history student is aware of the importance of primary sources, the original documents upon which any subsequent valid interpretation of history must be based. Volumes of old vellum and parchment were the *primary* primary sources from which much could be learned, not just from their subject matter, but also from basic physical properties, such as the material they were written on and in what kind of ink, and from the marginal comments that were added by later scribes and readers. They have much to teach us about the dreams and aspirations of those who wrote them. Even the fact of their preservation, often over centuries, is not accidental but the result of their symbolic value. No wonder that in many cases medieval manuscripts were the chief treasures of a church or monastery, to be copied and handed on for hundreds of years.

Nor is the influence of such manuscripts confined to the age that produced them. Biblical scholars, for example, still argue over ancient bits of papyrus and parchment, since even slight differences among early copies can deeply affect the subsequent teaching of the church. Medieval scholars argue about the reliability and even the genuineness of many manuscripts, since deciding on the correct "reading" or dating of a document can profoundly affect the quest for "what really happened," which, as the great nineteenth-century historian Otto von Ranke described, is the goal of all historical writing. In other words, these artifacts from the past continue to deeply affect how we see our own present, while pointing us toward the future.

This book takes a look at one such historical object, described in scholarly parlance as Corpus Christi College Manuscript 286. It is more popularly known as the St. Augustine Gospels. Produced in Rome in the late sixth century, and brought to England by St. Augustine of Canterbury, it is believed to be the oldest nonarcheological object in Great Britain and an important link in the history of the English Church. It also contains the earliest pictorial representation of the Last Supper in any manuscript. No wonder it is regarded as a national treasure—the oldest book in England. For seventy years it has been used as the Gospel book upon which each new archbishop of Canterbury takes the oath of office.

I first encountered this manuscript on a trip I made to England in 2010 to attend the Lambeth Conference as a bishop in the Episcopal Church. Since 1868, it has been the practice of the archbishop of Canterbury, the spiritual head of the Anglican Communion, to invite his fellow bishops to join him for a time of mutual reflection and prayer on the issues facing the 80 million Anglicans throughout the world. In earlier meetings, the bishops met at the archbishop's palace at Lambeth, across the Thames from Westminster Abbey. Now, with many more bishops, the venue has usually been a university campus, in our case the University of Kent near Canterbury.

As part of that visit, I joined my old friend, the Very Rev. Jeffrey John, dean of St. Alban's Cathedral, along with other bishops, on a trip to Cambridge to visit the colleges and museums there. One of the organizers of this trip, the Hon. Colin Colston, was apparently aware of my background as a medievalist, and he arranged for all of us to visit the Parker Library at Corpus Christi College and to meet its librarian, Dr. Christopher de Hamel.

Dr. de Hamel (whom you will get to know better later in this book) is not only one of the world's foremost experts on medieval Bibles, but also has a contagious enthusiasm for his subject. He invited us all to join him around a large table in the reading room of the library and placed before us a selection of documents related to English church history: letters from Henry VIII and Martin Luther, a Wycliffe Bible, the earliest copy of the *Anglo-Saxon Chronicle*, a Gospel book full of wonderful Celtic illuminations, even a record of the trial of Archbishop Thomas Cranmer with the bill for his last meal before he was burned at the stake in Oxford in 1556.

He saved the best for last. "We don't normally bring this out," he said. "But given that you are all bishops, I thought you would appreciate this last item. It is the oldest book in England, given to Augustine of Canterbury by the pope when he came to England in 597." We passed the manuscript around in great reverence, knowing that we were touching pages that Pope Gregory the Great and St. Augustine had once turned.

As you can imagine, as a former medievalist, I could hardly contain my enthusiasm in front of my fellow bishops. "Do you realize how lucky you are to see these things?" I asked. To the American bishops present I added, "This is as if we went to the National Archive in Washington, and the guards took the copy of the Constitution out of its bomb-proof vault and passed it around for us to handle!" My fellow bishops seemed only mildly interested, rather more concerned about missing lunch.

Although the days that followed were a once-in-a-lifetime experience—getting to meet with 700 bishops from around the world; having two days to be on retreat in Canterbury Cathedral, undisturbed by tourists; having dinner with then Archbishop Rowan Williams; and the highlight of every Lambeth Conference, tea with Queen Elizabeth at Buckingham Palace (along with 1,500 other guests!)—the pinnacle of my visit had been the few minutes that I had been able to hold Manuscript 286 in my hands. It is the only object we know of that St. Augustine must have handled and prayed over, the closest thing we Anglicans have to a relic of our founder.

As I reflected on that encounter, it began to occur to me that this manuscript was a symbol of many issues facing the church in our own day. It was first of all a product of mission. It had accompanied a man whose call was to bring the Good News of Jesus Christ to a distant and dangerous place. Surely it could serve as a reminder of our own need as a church today to become more mission-minded—concerned not so much with our own survival in a post-Christian world but in living up to our Great Commission of sharing the gospel with those who have never heard it.

But there was more to this ancient book. It represented a communications revolution in its own day. As one of the earliest examples of an illuminated book, it appropriated the visual arts into the toolbox of evangelism. As we in the church today struggle to adapt to the digital age and the opportunities that Facebook, Twitter, texting, and myriad other social media platforms provide, we can be reminded that in its own day, a picture of Jesus with his disciples on parchment was as revolutionary as a sermon podcast or an iPhone app.

The very survival of the St. Augustine Gospels also has important implications for us. Archbishop Matthew Parker, when he rescued this book from destruction at the time of the English Reformation, did so because he wanted to establish the continuity between the ancient church and the church of his own day. To that end, he assembled a collection of sources dealing with the early history of the church, a library of witnesses demonstrating that the newly created Church of England, of which he was the spiritual leader, was in fact the continuation of the church of the apostles. Parker valued continuity, as many still do. In fact, today we find many young people are intrigued with fresh expressions of ancient Christian practices, which provide them and us with continuity with the early church.

Christian bodies throughout the world share these quests for mission, effective communication, and continuity. Hence Manuscript 286 can also be for us a symbol of unity. It is no coincidence that Archbishop Rowan Williams had this manuscript brought to Westminster Cathedral during Pope Benedict's visit there in 2010 so that both leaders could venerate it together.

So I came to the idea that Manuscript 286, in addition to its historical value, possessed powerful symbolic significance for the Church today. With this in mind, I went back to the manuscript. Through the kind efforts of Dr. de Hamel, I was able to spend three days in the summer of 2012 in the company of the St. Augustine Gospels. What a privilege it was! As a doctoral student who was looking over my shoulder in the reading room remarked, "They don't bring that out for just anyone!"

In my time with the manuscript, I made a point of looking at every page and imagining how it might have been read and used. I am one of the lucky few to be able to spend such time with England's oldest book, and I want to share my thoughts and musings with you. The result is much more a meditation than a study.

Each chapter in this book—except the second, in which I describe the manuscript, its antecedents, and its later influence—is divided into two parts. The first part is descriptive of the Gospel book itself, while the second part uses the book as a departure point for reflection on issues facing the Church today. Hence the title, *Augustine's Relic: Lessons from the Oldest Book in England.* By "the Church" I mean especially the Episcopal Church in the United States as well as our sister churches in those provinces in the Anglican Communion who trace their origins to the efforts of St. Augustine and his mission to Anglo-Saxon England.

Everyone who is intrigued with history has at one time thought to him- or herself while looking at an artifact from the past, "If it could only talk!" Manuscript 286 continues to speak to us more than 1,400 years later, telling again the "old, old story"—not just of the Good News of Jesus but of the struggles of popes, missionaries, artists, archbishops, monks, and ordinary men and women to tell that story to the ends of the earth.

Acknowledgments

In the Middle Ages, the production of a book was always a group effort. In addition to providing the raw material and preparation of animal skins for vellum pages, ink, paint, gold leaf, leather, and wood, there was also a division of labor when it came to the actual writing. In a typical monastic scriptorium, one monk would prepare and rule the parchment while another would do the lettering, leaving space for a specialist to later add ornate capitals or illuminations.

This little book too would not have happened without the help and support of many. I am grateful to the Hon. Colin Colston for arranging my first visit to the Parker Library at Corpus Christi College, Cambridge, and to Dean Jeffrey John of St. Alban's and the Rev. Grant Holmes for providing me warm hospitality during my visits.

Crucial to this whole project was the help and support of Dr. Christopher de Hamel, librarian of the Parker Library, who not only provided me with access to the manuscript but was constantly available for help and suggestions. His assistant Gill Cannel was invaluable in locating documents while I was at the library and in arranging for the pictures that are included here. Taking time from their busy schedules, both Daniel Joslyn-Siemiatkoski and Elizabeth Drescher read my drafts and made many helpful suggestions.

It is hard to balance the job of being a bishop and finding time for writing, hence I am grateful to my staff at the Diocese of Arizona for helping organize my schedule to accomplish both and for cheering me on through the writing process. My editors at Church Publishing in New York, Nancy Bryan and Richard Bass, and the staff there were indispensable in getting the whole thing from computer to press.

The writing would have contained many more grammatical and stylistic errors had it not been for the capable proofreading of my helpmate and love of my life, Laura Fisher Smith. It is to her that I dedicate this little book.

Phoenix, Arizona
Feast of St. Augustine of Canterbury
May 26, 2015

— I —

Mission

Augustine was startled from his prayers by shouts of a crewman topside. Land! "*Deo gratias,*" murmured the monk as he clambered up the swaying rope ladder to get a look for himself. Although the crossing had been mercifully calm for this time of year, he could not wait to get ashore, even with his many anxieties of what might lie ahead. The air was sharp and cold as he raced to the rail. Low gray clouds lifted in places to reveal a sandy beach flanked by low dunes and a dark line of scrubby trees. There were no signs of life. Turning to either side, Augustine could see the masts of the two other small ships. At the prow of one he made out Brother Laurence shouting joyfully and waving his arms wildly. Many of the younger monks on that vessel seemed to be joining him in the celebration. He

spotted Brother Peter at the prow of the other ship, looking far more determined and grim, his face a mixture of
dread and determination.

Augustine's thoughts turned to his teacher and mentor,
Pope Gregory. He wished that somehow he could let the
Holy Father know that they had finally arrived. After all the
false starts, ecclesiastical intrigues, and physical hardships
along the way, his master's dream of a mission to the people
of this distant land, the *Angli,* was about to begin. While the
crew prepared to beach the ship on the shore, Augustine
began to inventory the supplies his small band of monks
and laborers would need upon landing.

They had been traveling light, depending upon the
goodwill of bishops and monasteries in Gaul to supply their
physical needs. Far more important than the casks of salted
fish and the cartons of hard dark bread, or the heavy wool
cloaks to wear over their black monks' habits, or even the
chests containing costly healing herbs and medicines, were
the treasured items they would need for the worship of God.
Augustine's thoughts turned to the heavy oaken chests, stowed
belowdecks, containing silver chalices and patens, rich bro-
cade stoles and chasubles to be worn during Mass, fair white
linen and brass candlesticks to adorn an altar. But most of all
he thought of the books—codices of the books of the Bible
written on parchment and bound in leather with iron clasps.
There were dozens of well-thumbed psalters and Bibles for
the monks to use for the Daily Offices, but there was also a
beautiful new book of Gospels decorated with pictures of the

four evangelists and scenes from the life of Jesus—a gift from Pope Gregory himself. Such a thing had hardly been seen in Rome, let alone in this most remote corner of the world. What a powerful object this would be for him and his men, a reminder of the Holy Father's commission to them, a symbol of the faith to impress the heathen population and a talisman as protection against their dark arts.

Augustine ran below to unpack Gregory's Gospel book from its silk-lined box. He called to one of his deacons. There was cargo to be unloaded, but first there was Mass to be said. He gave orders for a cross to be brought and for a piece of ship's planking to be set up as a table on the beach, between two large rocks. Clutching the Word of God to his chest, Augustine leapt from the boat into the shallow surf lapping the shore. His work as a missionary was about to begin. Who was Pope Gregory and why was he interested in sending a mission to England? Answering this question will provide us with the background we will need to understand MS 286.

There are only two popes who have had the title "the Great" added to their name. One of them is Gregory (540–604). For members of the Church of England and Anglican churches throughout the world, he is not simply great, he is the greatest, for without him, Canterbury would have remained a backwater and the history of Christianity in England would have been radically different.

Gregory became pope at a time when Europe was in disarray. The city of Rome itself was in ruins with once great imperial buildings slowly crumbling and sheep grazing in the forum from whence Roman emperors had once ruled the world. The last western Roman Emperor was Romulus Augustus, deposed by the Gothic warlord Odoacer in 476, but for decades before that the empire had begun to collapse from pressure from Germanic tribes on its northern borders, as well as internal corruption and conflict. Since the fourth century, Christianity had joined its fortunes with Imperial power, but in the East, under Byzantine control, the church had shrunk so much that by the time of Gregory, only parts of what are now France, Spain, and Italy were in communication with the bishop of Rome. The northern part of Europe was completely outside the Christian orbit, controlled by a host of barbarian and pagan tribes. One such area was the old Roman province of Britannia. Once controlled by Christian British peoples, it had been conquered by Germanic tribes from the east, except for the outlying regions of what are now Ireland, Scotland, and Wales, which managed to preserve their ancient Celtic and Christian culture.

Why then was Gregory so interested in England? Every English schoolchild has heard the story of Gregory's encounter with a group of fair-haired boys from Britain being sold as slaves in a Roman market. Impressed by their unusual light complexion, he inquired who they were and where they came from. The answer (in Latin of course) was that they were "*Angli*" (Angles). Gregory, not missing the opportunity to make a good pun, shot back, "*Non Angli sed Angeli*" (Not Angles but Angels). "Well named," he added, "for they have angelic faces and ought to be coheirs with the angels in heaven." And their origin? "*De Irei*" (from Ireland) was the answer. Gregory quipped that they certainly would be rescued "*de ira*" (from the wrath of God). Learning that the king of these Irish boys was named "*Aella*," he added, no doubt with a smile, "*Alleluia!*"[1]

This story has a ring of truth to it, even though it might have been embellished through the centuries. It is recounted by the most reliable historian of the early English Church, the seventh-century monk the Venerable Bede (of whom more later). And it reflects Gregory's passion for bringing the gospel to the frontiers of the known world.

Although this missionary zeal is the aspect of his pontificate that most concerns us here, Gregory was also one of the most competent and wise leaders of his age. Born about 540 to a noble Roman family of modest means with a tradition of civic service as well as strong family connections with the church (his great-great-grandfather was Pope Felix III), Gregory had an early exposure to the practical realities of church administration. But he was also deeply attracted to the idea of monasticism, and by the time he was about thirty he had turned his family mansion on the Caelian Hill (the "Beverly Hills" of the Rome of his day) over to a community of monks.

Interestingly, those monks commissioned a portrait of their benefactor shortly after his death, but it is now long lost. It was described by a ninth-century monastic visitor in words that give us an idea of what Gregory might have looked like. According to this account, Gregory was "rather bald" and had a "tawny" beard. His hair was long on the sides and carefully curled. His nose was "thin and straight" and "slightly aquiline." "His forehead was high." He had thick, "subdivided" lips and a chin "of a comely prominence" and "beautiful hands." This description influenced all subsequent portraits, from early icons to Carlo Saraseni's 1610 painting, which are consistent in portraying Gregory as thin, balding, and ascetic looking.[2]

From this community of monks would come the leaders of Gregory's missionary endeavors, and from his interest in the Benedictine model of community life would come his blueprint for how that work should be carried out. As much as the English Church owes its origin to the hard work and courage of Augustine of Canterbury, it owes even more to Augustine's mentor and model, Pope Gregory, provider of the vision and the resources for his mission, both spiritual and material.

In 590 Gregory began a papacy that is universally well regarded. He was even admired by the Protestant reformer John Calvin, for whom he was "the last of the good popes."[3] His career was distinguished by achievements in administration and organization and by his contribution to Christian theology. His massive *Moralia in Job,* with its method of allegorical interpretation of Scripture, was an intellectual staple throughout the Middle Ages, and his *Pastoral Care* is even now a valuable handbook of spiritual direction and still relevant to the duties of today's parish priest.

But Gregory's most important historical contribution was without doubt his advocacy and support of the English mission. His position as Peter's successor gave him the opportunity to fulfill the dream born of that early encounter in the slave market. So important to him was the project that he entrusted it to none other than a monk formed in the monastic community he founded in his own home—Augustine.

We know nothing about Augustine's background, nor of his mission, apart from what the historian Bede writes. And since Bede is our most important source for the English mission we are describing, it would be well to take a moment to examine his motives for writing.

Bede ("the Venerable" was added after his death in 735) is the most important source for early English history, but like all historians, his work was colored by his own agenda. His most famous work, *De historia ecclesiastica gentis Anglorum* (the *Ecclesiastical History of the English People*), written about 731, betrays its bias by its very title, the author's belief that a rather loose confederation of Germanic tribal chiefdoms somehow came to constitute a national entity—the English people. Bede spent his entire life as a monk at the important abbey of Wearmouth/Jarrow in Northumbria and writes very much from a "triumphalist" bias in which Gregory's mission serves as the starting point of God's divine plan to re-Christianize the English (meaning the Anglo-Saxon inhabitants of southern and eastern England). When it comes to failures and setbacks, or to personalities that don't fit into his design, Bede tends to gloss over them. Still, Bede has justly earned the title of the "Father of English History" for the completeness of his work, his efforts to use available past sources (his monastery had an excellent library), and above all for his willingness to seek out eyewitnesses, unusual for writers of his time. Indeed, he boasts that he "relies on the faithful testimony of innumerable witnesses"[4] and is not afraid to name names. One such witness was Albinus, the abbot of the monastery in Canterbury, who provided much early documentation. Another was Nothhelm, later to be an archbishop of Canterbury but at the time of Bede's writing a priest in London, who had obtained copies of Gregory the Great's correspondence from Rome relating to Augustine's mission.

Gregory and Augustine were the heroes of Bede's not always unbiased account. Their motivation for the mission to England was clear to him—to spread the gospel. Some "decontructionist" historians have speculated that Gregory might have had more Machiavellian motives for dispatching Augustine to England. The Lombards had taken over parts of Italy, and Gregory could have used an English mission as a counterweight to what he considered to be their barbarian and heretical influence. Perhaps he was looking for a toehold in England to balance the power of the bishops in Gaul (France). Or he might have seen this mission as a way of bringing the surviving British or Celtic bishops under his sway. Just as his twentieth-century successor Pope John Paul

II looked to Poland and middle Europe as fertile ground for a rebirth of the church in our time, so Gregory saw the future of the Roman Church in his own day as lying with the barbarian-occupied countries of the west—what is now England, Ireland, and the Spanish peninsula. His youthful sojourn in Greece as an *apocrisiarius* (a form of ambassador from the papal to the imperial court) left him impressed with both the vitality and spirituality of the Eastern Church and gave him a vision of what the Western Church could be.

Yet most modern historians conclude that Gregory's motives for mission were pure—to spread the gospel to the ends of the world. Indeed, Gregory's own theology saw this as a necessary step to ushering in the end-time and Christ's Second Coming. Gregory believed that the end of the world was imminent and that he, as spiritual leader of Christendom, was destined to play a major part in God's plan for the coming apocalypse. His belief was rooted in the prevalent notion that the world would go through six ages, and that he was living at the end of the last of these. This helps explain Gregory's decision to dispatch his mission to Anglo-Saxon Britain, since conversion of the heathen was an important requirement for the Second Coming (see, for example, Matt. 24:14). And so, in addition to his efforts in England, Gregory also encouraged other missionary endeavours. Arians and Jews in Italy were targeted for conversion, along with heathen populations in Sicily and Sardinia.

So great was Gregory's desire to undertake a major mission that Bede reports that even from the time he was elected pope,

Gregory planned on traveling to England himself, although the citizens of Rome refused to let him go. "It is true that he sent other preachers, but he himself helped their preaching to bear fruit through his encouragement and prayers."[5]

Early in his pontificate Gregory wrote to one of the papal estate managers in southern Gaul asking that he buy English slave boys in order that they be educated in monasteries. This might be an indication that Gregory was already planning the mission to Britain at that time and that he intended to send the slaves as missionaries. We might rightly wonder if Augustine himself was a former British slave, chosen for his knowledge of the mission territory and ability to speak the language.

Gregory probably had a fairly accurate idea of what Augustine would face when he arrived on English shores. For more than two hundred years, the southern part of England had been in the hands of descendants of Anglo-Saxon invaders who had gradually displaced the Romano-British population. So, in addition to his religious goals, Gregory would no doubt have welcomed the chance to reestablish Roman hegemony over what had originally been the farthest northern border of the Roman Empire.

Much of the Romano-British population at the time was Christian, having been converted by settlers from the rest of Christianized Europe. Very little is known about these early British Christians. There are sketchy references to some British bishops who attended the Council of Arles in 452, and one of the most famous of the early heretics, Pelagius

(354–420), was himself a British native. (Some would even argue that Pelagianism, summed up in the gross simplification, "God helps those who help themselves," still plays a role in English theological thinking!)

The Anglo-Saxon conquering tribes were, however, pagans, and we do know a considerable amount about their customs and religion, thanks to the work of early historians and to important archeological discoveries, such as the treasure trove discovered at the Sutton Hoo royal burial site in the 1930s. When imagining early Anglo-Saxon culture, one may think "Vikings," since they were closely related both in language and culture. They worshipped the same Norse gods who have given their names to the days in our week: *Twi* (Tuesday), *Woden* (Wednesday), *Thunor* or *Thor* (Thursday), *Frige* (Friday). And they shared a common culture and economy, as is evident in such early literary works as the great epic poem *Beowulf.*

Following the withdrawal of Roman troops around 410, these Anglo-Saxon tribes from northern Germany and Friesland began to displace the native population through invasion and assimilation. As these pagan settlements took over, the native British Church was pushed west and north into the areas of Wales, Scotland, and Ireland, and consequently evolved in isolation from Rome. This native church developed its own distinctive culture centered on monasteries instead of bishoprics. Other distinguishing characteristics were its calculation of the date of Easter and the style of the tonsure, or haircut, that clerics wore. This

"Celtic Christianity" was to play its own important role in English church history and would eventually interact with the Roman version brought to England by Augustine. What is important to note is that there is no evidence that these native British Christians tried to convert their Anglo-Saxon conquerors. That task would be left to Augustine and his band of Roman missionaries.

It was toward a southern tribe of these Anglo-Saxons that Gregory targeted his re-Christianization efforts. The area of Kent was ruled by Aethelbert (560–616), one of the most powerful Anglo-Saxon chieftain-kings. Bede states that his overlordship extended as far north as the river Humber, a huge chunk of territory. Much more importantly, Aethelbert was married to Bertha, the daughter of the Frankish King Cheribert I, part of the Merovingian dynasty that ruled what is now northern France.

Bertha was a Christian and had thus been allowed to bring with her into the marriage settlement a Frankish bishop by the name of Luidhard to serve as her chaplain. Together the two of them rebuilt several places of Christian worship in and around the ancient Roman settlement of *Durovernum*—in that day called *Cantwaraburh,* what would become Canterbury. One such place is the lovely little parish church of St. Martin, located within walking distance of Canterbury Cathedral, widely agreed to be the oldest place of Christian worship in England still functioning as a parish church. Although the structure has been rebuilt many times, Roman-style red bricks are still visible in its walls.

Strangely, Luidhard didn't seem to make much of an impact on the Kentish subjects whose Queen he served, and we would probably know nothing about him at all except for the accidental find in the nineteenth century of a coin with his name and likeness on it. If he died as early as 590, as some believe, the vacancy he left might have served as yet another incentive for Gregory to intervene. Bede, however, implies that Luidhard was still alive when Augustine arrived in 597, and there has been recent archaeological evidence from the Canterbury area that indicates that Bertha and Luidhard were likely not the only Christians in the area.

By 595, Gregory was ready to dispatch Augustine, who was accompanied by other monks. Lawrence, his eventual successor at Canterbury, is the only one we know by name among about forty others, including some Frankish translators. Gregory smoothed the way for his band of missionaries by writing to several of the Frankish bishops, asking for their support and hospitality. Yet despite Gregory's efforts to insure an easy journey for Augustine, the travelers had hardly left Roman territory before their fears overwhelmed them and they turned back. Bede reports that they "were paralysed with terror" at the prospect of "going to a barbarous, fierce, and unbelieving nation whose language they did not even understand."[6] Here we sense that Augustine, although he might have been learned and reasonably capable as a monastic administrator, was somewhat lacking in both vision and courage, for the trip was not particularly arduous, and, as we have seen, he could have expected to be greeted at least civilly if not warmly as a representative of the pope in the territories through which he had to travel.

Gregory, however, was not to be deterred and refused to let Augustine off the hook. He sent him back with a stern letter enjoining him and his companions to finish the task they had started and not be put off by fear of the journey or "the tongues of evil speakers." This last phrase suggests that Augustine may have faced a mutiny of sorts among his missionary team.

Resuming their itinerary, they made their way slowly northward through Gaul, stopping for refreshment at such places as Tours before making the Channel crossing in the spring of 597. Bede reports that he made land at Thanet, which was at that time an island, and served as an important beacon or navigation point for boats making the Channel crossing (the name comes from the Celtic word for "high fire" or beacon).

Aethelbert kept them on the island for a while "until he had decided what to do with them." After a few days, he received them there and granted them permission to live among his subjects, since he was convinced that "they had come to share with them things good and true." He promised to support them and permitted them "to win all you can by your faith and by your preaching."[7]

Aethelbert, either because of his own religious beliefs or because he thought it would be politically astute, met the missionaries for that first interview in the open air, since it was believed that magic was less effective outdoors, and that should Augustine prove to be a sorcerer, his powers would be limited there.

So the mission was off to a good start. Aethelbert provided a place for them to live in his royal palace in Canterbury. When they were allowed to enter Canterbury, we can easily imagine Augustine and his companions making their way into Aethelbert's compound, dressed in their monastic habits, chanting psalms and carrying a silver cross and a large panel picture of Jesus as well as books and liturgical objects they would have needed.

The most important victory for the early missionaries was the baptism of King Aethelbert himself, which may have taken place as early as that first year, although the literary evidence is conflicting. Aethelbert may not have originally intended to be baptized, thinking that he could simply use Augustine to gain access to the distant pope in Rome, thus giving himself some political leverage against the Franks on the other side of the Channel. So it is to Augustine's credit that his message was initially so compelling.

Still, some historians of this period have cautioned against any triumphalist assumptions. The fortunes of Gregory's mission depended heavily on the support of Aethelbert, which means that its successes were limited, as we shall see. One writer has commented that the monastic community at Canterbury more resembled "a cordoned-off residence of privileged foreigners—valuable but potentially disruptive persons, best kept under surveillance and answerable to the royal court—than it did the extensive network of established Roman bishoprics that Gregory had planned."[8]

Bede of course paints a more positive picture. For him, the success of this venture was proved first by the baptism of Aethelbert and then by the spreading influence of Christianity in the area and the establishment of local mission stations and schools. Shortly after his arrival, Augustine was designated bishop for the English by Pope Gregory, although he may have actually been consecrated by bishops in Gaul during his trip. It wasn't long before he had established a monastic foundation in Canterbury. It is unclear whether the monks followed the Benedictine rule, although this seems likely given Gregory's fondness for the Benedictine ethos. Less probable was any kind of mass conversion of the English people or the kind of exaggerated successes that Bede reports. We can instead imagine a slow and steady influence that came through education, worship, and reforming churches and Christian communities in an area that had survived the earlier pagan onslaughts and established a kind of low-level peaceful coexistence with their Anglo-Saxon overlords.

It was not long after settling in that Augustine was directed by the pope to return to Gaul to be ordained archbishop of the "English Race" (*gens Anglorum*) by the archbishop of Arles. His new status was symbolized by the gift of the pallium, the special lambswool collar given by the pope as a symbol of metropolitan or archiepsicopal status. It can still be seen in the coat of arms of the archbishops of Canterbury.

Shortly after his return from Gaul, Augustine reported back to Gregory and posited to the pope a series of questions, which his master dutifully answered. These guidelines, referred to as the *Libellus responsionum,* or "Little Answer Book," were extracted into Bede's account and focus on such topics as the consecration of additional bishops, sexual behavior as it relates to church membership, marriage guidelines, and punishment for church crimes.

Throughout the *Libellus,* Gregory takes a rather hardline position: Augustine is to enforce the practices of the Church in Rome. However, a short time later, in the so-called *Epistola ad Mellitum,* also referenced by Bede, Gregory shifted his attitude toward greater inclusion and accommodation. So, for example, he tells Augustine that temples dedicated to pagan idols should be reconsecrated to Christian worship:

> I have decided . . . that the idol temples of the [English] race should by no means be destroyed, but only the idols in them. Take holy water and sprinkle it in these shrines, build altars and place relics in them. For if the shrines are well built, it is essential that they should be changed from the worship of devils [*cultu daemonum*] to the service of the one true God.[9]

This practice of "despoiling the Egyptians"—adapting pagan customs to Christian practice—was to be a hallmark of successful Christian missionary activity ever after.

One of Gregory's goals for Augustine was to make contact with the surviving bishops of the British church and to bring them back under Roman control. This assignment did not go well. The Celtic church leaders gathered at a border location to consider the proposal put before them. If they would agree to celebrate Easter according to the Roman calendar, baptize according to the Roman rite, and work together with Augustine's mission to evangelize the heathen, they could keep the rest of their native ways. According to Bede, when the delegates withdrew to consider this proposal, they were advised by one of their holy men to first determine if Augustine was a true servant of Christ. This they would know if, when they came into his presence, Augustine humbly rose to greet them. If he did not, they would know him to be arrogant and not worthy of their respect. Augustine failed the test: "Now it happened that Augustine remained seated while they were coming in; when they saw this, they forthwith became enraged, and setting him down as a proud man, strove to contradict everything he said."[10] Augustine, for his part, called down God's wrath on them for their lack of cooperation, a prophetic act according to Bede, who felt that the Celtic church leaders paid for this heresy when they were later massacred in a battle by the Saxon King Aethelfrith.

Despite Augustine's lack of political tact, as well as Gregory's underestimation of the willingness of the native British church to be reassimilated under his control, the pope was impressed enough to expand the foothold he had gained in England. Thus in 601 he sent reinforcements to Augustine in the form of churchly hardware, vestments, and books. If our manuscript was not in the original group of "codici" of 596, it would have been in this newest cache of supplies.

Along with the pallium, a letter from Gregory directed the new archbishop to ordain twelve suffragan or assisting bishops as soon as possible and to send a bishop to York. Gregory's apparent plan was for two archbishops, one at York and one at London, with twelve suffragan bishops under each archbishop. As part of this plan, Augustine was expected to transfer his archiepiscopal see to London from Canterbury. The move from Canterbury to London never happened; no contemporary sources give the reason, but it was most likely because London was not part of Aethelbert's domain but was part of the kingdom of Essex and belonged to Aethelbert's nephew Saebert, who had not yet converted to Christianity.

Regardless of Bede's sometimes breathless account of the successes of Gregory's mission to England, Augustine's efforts were short-lived. Because his missionary work was so connected with the rule of Aethelbert, its scope did not extend much beyond the range of the immediate area around Canterbury, although before his death in 604, Augustine did manage to consecrate two new bishops, Mellitus (d. 624) for London (he would eventually become the third archbishop of Canterbury) and Justus (d. 631) for Rochester. He also provided for his own succession by appointing Laurentius (Lawrence) (d. 619) to take his place in Canterbury. But by the early part of the seventh century most of these efforts had come to naught. Paulinus (d. 644), the first bishop of York, was forced to retreat south when pagan reaction to his work drove him out in 633.

Despite such setbacks, Augustine planted seeds that were to produce much fruit. He founded a school in Canterbury and introduced Roman liturgical practice, Mediterranean culture and architecture, and the Benedictine model of monastic life to the Anglo-Saxon areas of England. As the political situation began to stabilize around the later seventh century and more regional kings were baptized, the stage was set for a flowering of Christian culture epitomized by figures like Bede. The early Anglo-Saxon church produced a confident missionary style of its own that was eventually exported to Gaul and Germany by men like Willibrord (d. 739) and Boniface (d. 754).

Gregory's mission to England did not exactly turn out as he had hoped. Although there were remnants of the old Romano-British church still in place, these were not nearly as strong as Gregory had anticipated. Nor did Augustine's failure to cooperate with the remaining British bishops help matters. Still there is much we can learn from Gregory's missionary efforts that can be applied to our own church and its desire to preach the gospel "to the ends of the earth."

First and foremost, Gregory was motivated by a sincere desire to spread the Good News. Even though he must have been aware of the geopolitical advantages that a Romanized

Christian outpost would provide, Gregory was steeped in a theology in which the preaching of Christ was intimately connected with his Second Coming. Gregory clearly saw himself as an instrument in this salvation history and was thus compelled to do everything his position allowed him to do to save souls.

Because this task was eschatological in nature, it carried with it a sense of urgency. Gregory's proactive strategizing and deliberate planning mark not only a departure from his beloved Benedictine heritage but also one of the earliest large-scale missionary efforts directed at a certain people in a certain place. Up to this point, the church tended to accomplish conversion by example. Holy men and women would establish themselves in a locality and then bring others to faith through modeling and persuasion. The construction of a monastery would influence a local area. The process tended to be individualist, low key, and loosely organized. One thinks of some of the effective missionary efforts in Europe before Augustine's time, such as Martin of Tours or Patrick of Ireland. Gregory's commissioning of Augustine had characteristics of a military campaign, with advance planning, instructions from headquarters, and organized logistical support. It was deliberate, organized, and efficient.

Gregory also understood the necessity of "ministry on the fringes." He rightly surmised that large-scale conversion often takes place on the borders, among those who are outside the mainstream of society. This tendency was inherent in the church from its beginnings, when the Apostle Paul realized that Gentile "God-fearers" were ripe for evangelization and were far readier to hear the message of Jesus than his own Jewish culture. For Gregory, England must have been truly the *ultima Thule* of his day, a heathen place with strange customs and a stranger language.

The flexibility demonstrated by Gregory in his *Epistola ad Mellitum,* in which he encouraged Augustine and his successors to adapt the Christian message to local conditions, stands as a fundamental tenet of any effective missionary endeavor. This emphasis is far more than a pragmatic solution to local situation. It is not just about building churches on the sites of pagan temples or metamorphosing pagan feasts into Christian holy days. It has to do with an openness to the dominant culture, appropriating what is potentially helpful to the larger goal. It also meant as a willingness to train indigenous clergy and to place them in positions of authority. It was less than two generations after Augustine's arrival that a native Anglo-Saxon (Deusdedit, in Anglo-Saxon, Frithona, d. 664) succeeded him as archbishop of Canterbury. Before that, Ithamar (d. ca. 655) had been consecrated bishop of Rochester in 644. Such willingness to recruit native leaders helped to insure the mission's eventual success.

Finally, Gregory acknowledged the need for an underlying structure to conduct mission. He provided the logistical support that was needed in the form of manpower (at least forty monks and translators), equipment (those vestments, vessels, and books mentioned by Bede), local support (the bishops in Gaul), and the considerable amount of money and supplies that it must have required to transport the participants to the shores of Kent, not to mention his own considerable ongoing instruction and support. All this to bring the gospel to England.

What can Gregory's passion for mission mean for us in the church today?

Gregory was clear in his goal for sending Augustine to Britain: Convert the Anglo Saxons he found there to Christianity. It goes without saying that he was following the Great Commission: "Go therefore and make disciples of all nations, baptizing them in the name of the Father and of the Son and of the Holy Spirit" (Matt. 28:19).

Such are Jesus's words at the end of the Gospel of Matthew. They are words that resonated with the actions of Jesus's followers at the launching of the mission of the church in the book of Acts. Before his Ascension, Jesus promises his disciples: "But you will receive power when the Holy Spirit has come upon you; and you will be my witnesses in Jerusalem, in all Judea and Samaria, and to the ends of the earth" (Acts 1:8).

That being a follower of Jesus also meant being a missionary committed to spreading the Christian message of God's care and redemption was the central thesis of the work of the greatest missionary of all time, St. Paul, whose tireless travels through much of the ancient Western world brought him eventually to Rome and martyrdom. The Good News that Paul announced was God's saving action made known in the death and resurrection of Jesus Christ, and it was a message for everyone to hear:

> For there is no distinction between Jew and Greek; the same Lord is Lord of all and is generous to all who call on him. For, "Everyone who calls on the name of the Lord shall be saved." But how are they to call on one in whom they have not believed? And how are they to believe in one of whom they have never heard? And how are they to hear without someone to proclaim him? And how are they to proclaim him unless they are sent? As it is written, "How beautiful are the feet of those who bring good news!" (Rom. 10:12–15)

It was this impulse toward mission, this passion for sharing the Good News of Jesus Christ, that energized a handful of uneducated and unsophisticated disciples to spiritually and intellectually conquer the Mediterranean world in a little more than two hundred years.

What seemed clear to Gregory has often been forgotten in our own day. The church has lost touch with its missionary heritage. Through its history the church has experienced periods of great missionary expansion. One thinks, for example, of the Roman Catholic efforts in the New World in the fifteenth and sixteenth centuries, the work of the Church of

England in the American colonies in the eighteenth century, or the expansion of European Protestant churches into the continents of Asia and Africa in the nineteenth century. But for most first-world Christians since then, much of that missionary impulse has been lost as complex factors have forced churches to concentrate more on survival than on expansion. Across modern denominations there is even a lack of clarity of exactly what constitutes the content of the Good News. What, for example, should we do with Jesus's claim that he is "the way, the truth, and the life" (John 14:6) in a culturally and religiously pluralistic world? Does God's plan of salvation include Muslims, Jews, and well-meaning secular humanists? Perhaps closer to home for most practicing churchgoers are such questions as: How do we even speak of our faith to others, and do we in fact have any obligation to do so? What is the purpose of the institutional church—to equip its members for mission or to maintain a comfortable pew for those already attending? Often when as bishop I visit congregations I pose the question, "What is the purpose of your congregation; why did God put you here?" The answers I am likely to receive go along the lines of, "To stay open," "So I can have a place to see my friends," or even, "It's a nice place to go before brunch!"

Christians of all denominations are wrestling with the question, "What is the mission of the church?" not just because the answer is vital to our theological identity and understanding, but for the more practical reason that in the first world, institutional Christianity is in sharp decline.

This reality forces congregations to close or seriously curtail their ministry, and shrinking revenues push local congregations to cut back or eliminate programs that served their own neighborhood or supported schools, clinics, and feeding programs around the world. The church in most Western countries is not even holding its own in terms of membership or finances, let alone growing or expanding.

Yet the news has not been all bad. In the third world, Christianity has seen explosive growth, although often not in forms most Westerners would recognize. Moreover, there is intense interest in spiritual topics, especially among young people, who are more likely than their elders to identify as "spiritual but not religious." They can be found walking the labyrinth or registering for monastic retreats, taking pilgrimage treks or holding a Bible study session in Starbucks, even though they are unlikely to ever darken the door of a church building on Sunday morning.

Some of this energy has resulted in the exploration of new ways of being the church—sometimes referred to as the emergent church in America or as the Fresh Expressions movement in Great Britain—experimental ways of recasting the ancient Christian proclamation in new cultural forms.

Such new energy both within and without the established church has in turn fostered a new emphasis on the mission of church. What is it, and how should it be practiced? Can we even use the term "mission" without conjuring up images of nineteenth-century colonial missionaries exploiting native populations at the same time they sought to save their souls? As we shall see, this discussion can be much informed by the example of earlier missionaries such as St. Augustine of Canterbury.

A serious official attempt to define the mission of the church in the twenty-first century began with the 2004 publication of the archbishop of Canterbury's *Mission-Shaped Church*.[11] This study revisited the Church of England's strategy for growth, which had not been seriously discussed for a generation. It first took stock of our culture (postmodern and post-Christian), reformulated a theology of mission ("The church is the fruit of the mission of God"), and made suggestions on how to proceed by creating "fresh expressions of the church"—ways in which the church could take the gospel message to people where they are, both geographically and culturally, rather than expecting them to come to church.

This study was enormously popular and has sold thousands of copies. Even a decade later, it has set the tone for subsequent discussion for what has often been termed the "emergent" or future church. Rethinking the church's mission and calling for structural changes has spawned an enormous body of literature beyond the scope of this study. However, most attempts focus on three areas: (1) taking stock of a radically changed cultural milieu, (2) restating mission as something initiated by God rather than the church, and (3) imagining a deinstitutionalized future for the church. Let's look at each of these three themes briefly in turn:

This Is Not Your Grandfather's Pew might be a good a title for a new book about the emergent church. Like most studies in this genre, it would begin with a catalog of the way the church failed to respond to the cultural changes of the past few decades, resulting in catastrophic loss of membership, especially in those Christian denominations that used to be referred to as "mainline"—Presbyterians, Methodists, Congregationalists, Episcopalians, and others. The decline in these denominations has been so great that some critics suggest that they might be better termed "old line" or even "sidelined" churches! For example, in the Episcopal Church, membership loss is roughly the equivalent of one diocese per year. At this rate, church demographers are not overstating the facts when they warn that the Episcopal Church will cease to exist within two generations. Some of these demographers forecast a "Tsunami of Death" that has just now begun to affect local congregations, although we can get a glimpse of its effects if we merely count the number of those on Sunday morning who have either gray hair or none at all!

The explanations for this decline are many: a low birthrate among members of these particular denominations, a distrust of all institutions dating from the cultural upheavals of the 1960s, the breakdown in family and social structures as the result of easy divorce and accessible contraception, a post–Second World War explosion of materialism and consumerism, and the corrosive effects of television and mass entertainment. One obvious "fail" likely to head the list of most studies (and a topic we will return to in the chapter on communication) is the reluctance of the established churches to respond to digital technology and social media. While most of the world is living in a world where instant communication, visual presentation, and social networking are taken for granted, the institutional church for the most part is stuck in a nineteenth-century world in which the printed word, dry oral presentations (sermons), and hymns written by "dead white guys" accompanied by organs are still the norm.

Culturally too, the perception—if not the reality—of American Christianity is that it is politically reactionary, homophobic, and judgmental, more interested in maintaining its own structures than it is proclaiming the essentially countercultural message of the gospel. Indeed it has even been suggested that "the mission of the church is paying the clergyman." No wonder young people give the institutional church wide berth!

But even if the demographic reality is bleak, there are those who are actively re-visioning the mission of the church in language that moves it away from its moribund and self-serving expressions and into alignment with the larger purposes of God. Key to this movement is an insight provided by the archbishop's report that distinguishes between the mission of the church (*missio ecclesiae*) and the mission of God (*missio Dei*). In the past, Christians were called upon to support the work or mission of the church; the institution set the agenda. In this model "successful mission" could be evaluated by such metrics as number of conversions, congregations planted, or church buildings constructed. In the new theology of mission, the emphasis is not on what we in the church are doing, but what God is already doing in our communities. God is always one step ahead of us, at work in places and among people who normally would not even be associated with the church. David Bosch, quoting the theologian Jurgen Moltmann, sums it up:

> Mission is not primarily an activity of the Church, but an attribute of God. God is a missionary God. "It is not the church that has a mission of salvation to fulfill in the world; it is the mission of the Son and the Spirit through the Father, and it includes the church." . . . There is church because there is mission, not vice versa. The church must not think its role is identical to the *missio Dei*; the church is participating in the mission of God. The church's mission is a subset of a larger whole mission. That is, it is part of God's mission to the world and not the entirety of God's work in the world.[12]

From this theological assumption, a new way of doing church emerges, which might be described as a "Road to Emmaus" approach in which Christians "walk alongside" people in their communities. Instead of elbowing their way into communities, buying land, putting up buildings, announcing times of services, and doing everything they can to attract customers to their franchised version of the Christian faith, the church makes a point of building relationships rather than selling prepackaged answers. Whereas the "old school" model for the church was "build it and they will come," it now should be, "we will come to you."

There are plenty of examples of the success of this approach. A clergy couple runs a community center and preschool in one of the poorest sections of Chicago; a parish day school holds a Sunday worship service for parents; a group of twenty-somethings move from affluent Scottsdale to downtown Phoenix in order to start a Christian coffeehouse and community in an abandoned warehouse; a young priest in Los Angeles holds a prayer service in the middle of "Needle Park" and eventually organizes the community to form a successful industrial cleaning company.

This theology of mission assumes that God's work is especially present where Christ was present in his earthly ministry—on the fringes of society, among those who are poor, neglected, oppressed, or otherwise forgotten. This is why the institutional types (Sadducees and Pharisees) were always the recipients of Jesus's most scathing criticisms. As Rowan Williams points out, "Jesus is always asking us to associate with people we would rather avoid."[13] This is why mission is always outwardly focused and always directed to those who are on the edges of society.

Such a new, emergent approach to the theology of mission will take some getting used to. For most churchgoers, talk of "mission" usually conjures up images of nineteenth-century white European missionaries wearing pith helmets and "saving souls" in darkest Africa. This kind of cultural chauvinism, which often included forcing native peoples to wear pants as well as read the Bible, has been rightly rejected as part of a colonialist agenda, yet most of the faithful are unclear as to what comes in its place. The Book of Common Prayer reflects this vague attitude. There are several collects mentioning Christian mission, although most of them portray it as a rather passive affair, something which has already happened. In thanking God for missionaries, defined as "those whom you have sent in the power of the Spirit to preach the Gospel to all nations," their work is described as a *fait accompli*. "We thank you that in all parts of the earth a community of love has been gathered together by their prayers and labors, and that in every place your servants call upon your Name."[14] Really? This assumption of "mission accomplished" would no doubt be a surprise to those living in many places in the Middle East or Asia, let alone the cities of the United States.

Whose task is it then to preach the gospel? The Prayer Book seems to imply that we believers are off the hook. It is God's responsibility to convert, while we can sit idly by:

> O God, you have made of one blood all the peoples of the earth, and sent your blessed Son to preach peace to those who are far off and to those who are near: Grant that people everywhere may seek after you and find you, bring the nations into your fold, pour out your Spirit upon all flesh, and hasten the coming of your kingdom.[15]

Sounds like any conversion work to be done is up to God! At best, the work of evangelism is to be left to extraordinary individuals. So on the feast day of a missionary, instead of asking God that we all might be blessed with similar zeal, we beseech God to "raise up in this and every land evangelists and heralds of your Kingdom, that your Church may proclaim the unsearchable riches of our Savior Jesus Christ."[16] The best attempt to energize all the faithful comes in another collect for mission where it is acknowledged that there are still those who "have not known the redeeming work of our Savior Jesus Christ," and that it is now "by the prayers and labors of your holy Church, they might be brought to know and worship you as you have been revealed in your Son."[17] The catechism at the back of the Prayer Book (*terra incognita* for most worshipers) is perhaps the only place that the mission of the church includes all believers for "the Church carries out its mission through the ministry of all its members."[18]

Overall, however, one gets the impression from the catechism that spreading the Good News is not really an expectation of discipleship and that the vocation of all faithful people is confined to "truly and devoutly serve [God]."[19]

Are we simply to ignore the call to "share the Good News" and opt for an inwardly focused spirituality? Is bringing people to Christ something only "evangelistic" churches do? Is putting up a welcome sign enough or do we need to go door to door?

One helpful answer to these questions can be found in *Reclaiming the Great Commission,* a book by the former bishop of Texas, Claude Payne. The thesis is simple: The church needs to set aside such issues as sexuality and structure and return to its core value of sharing the gospel in all that it does—summarized in Jesus's Great Commission to his followers at the end of Matthew's Gospel. Bishop Payne was not content to simply outline a blueprint for church renewal. He dedicated many hours of his retirement to recruiting a cadre of up-and-coming young clergy leaders who shared his philosophy and sought in their own ministries to move the church "from maintenance to mission."

This change in the *zeitgeist* (or the *Heilige Geist*) of the church is reflected in the Church of England in the Fresh Expressions movement, the Greenbelt gathering, and other groups as clergy and laity who have rediscovered a new way of doing evangelism, motivated not by fear but by attraction to a new way of living out one's baptismal call.

The result is that even in the midst of an overall membership decline in the wider church, there are glimpses of hope as new generation of leaders in the church commit themselves to "mission shaped" congregations and dioceses. It would seem that author Phyllis Tickle's observation is right, that we are in the midst of a "Great Emergence" in which the church "holds a rummage sale every 500 years" and essentially recreates itself.

Gregory' s mission to Kent is perhaps the earliest example of the church targeting an entire population for conversion. In that sense his intentionally large-scale missionary activities represent the kind of historical innovation that Tickle sees periodically emerging throughout church history. In the mission entrusted to his friend St. Augustine, we can detect some themes common to any evangelization movement that can still inform us today as we rediscover the importance of mission to the life of the church.

THE MISSION OF THE CHURCH REQUIRES
A CLEAR SENSE OF PURPOSE

The sixth-century Western church was blessed to have a leader like Gregory who possessed both the vision and the organizational skills to launch his work in Britain. His clear mandate to save the souls of the *angeli* he had seen in the slave market of Rome was further fueled by an apocalyptic fervor that convinced him converting the heathen would hasten the Second Coming. Gregory combined this compelling vision with a keen grasp of European *realpolitik*. He knew he needed the support of the Frankish bishops for Augustine's beachhead in Kent to succeed, and he got it. He counted on the welcome of Bertha and her small group of Christians already in Kent, and he got that too.

Sadly, as we have seen, our church today often lacks such a clearly defined purpose. The Anglican Consultative Council meeting in 1984 realized the need for this clear focus, at least in theory, and published a list of the "Five Marks of Mission," which could serve as signposts for a way forward:

1. To proclaim the Good News of the kingdom
2. To teach, baptize, and nurture new believers

3. To respond to human need by loving service
4. To seek to transform unjust structures of society
5. To strive to safeguard the integrity of creation and sustain and renew the life of the earth[20]

Unfortunately, the church does not often practice what it preaches. So, for example, at its 2012 General Convention, the Episcopal Church's influential committee on program, budget, and finance adopted the Five Marks of Mission as its guideline in its budgeting process, and then largely ignored these imperatives, especially the first two, instead shoring up programs and offices that have proved in many cases to be ineffective. Efforts made at the recent 2015 gathering were much more positive, with an unprecedented amount of funding being directed toward church planting and evangelism.

Gregory's ability to focus on "making the main thing the main thing," namely proclaiming the Gospel to those who had never heard it, and his refusal to be distracted from that goal, accounted for his missionary success. This is the first lesson we must learn from the oldest book in England, which after all, is a collection of the four Gospels!

THE MISSION OF THE CHURCH TAKES PLACE ON THE MARGINS OF SOCIETY

Julius Caesar invaded Britain in 55 BCE, and it had become part of the Roman Empire. Although the Romano-British church had reached a high degree of development, even to the point of being represented at the Council of Nicea in 325, there was little left of Christianity in Britain after the Germanic pagan invasions of the fifth and sixth centuries. As we have seen, it is likely that there were small enclaves of practicing Christians even in places like Canterbury before Augustine's arrival. Queen Bertha had her own chaplain, and some sort of worship was taking place at St. Martin's Church just to the east of Ethelbert's settlement. Still, the Anglo-Saxon kingdoms were *terra incognita* to the rest of the Mediterranean world. Anglo-Saxon warriors had a reputation as fierce fighters. Dressed in their animal skins and horned helmets, beards and long flowing hair, it is no wonder that they struck fear into the Britons they either conquered or drove west and north into Wales, Scotland, and Cornwall in the course of their long series of invasions. Augustine, it will be remembered, was so frightened by the reputation of those whose souls he was sent to save that he turned back to Rome and had to be given a pep talk by Gregory before setting out again.

Anglo-Saxon Britain was truly the "ends of the earth" in the ancient world, populated by people whose language and culture was utterly foreign to late Roman civilization. Our modern world has its own such divisions. Although geographical frontiers have disappeared for us, there are still many segments of our populations that are in the periphery of established Christian churches' vision. They are not located in distant lands, but are right here among us. Such groups—which are underrepresented among the ranks of most churches, the Episcopal Church in particular—include:

- **Youth.** In the United States, the vast majority of young people have no involvement in any church. In fact, something like two-thirds have never been inside a church building! I suspect that figure is even higher for Great Britain and much of Europe. The causes for this age gap in church statistics are complicated; some of them will be touched upon later throughout this book. Still, even among this unchurched population of young people, there is tremendous interest in spirituality and even in the message of Jesus. (One college chaplain reports that he often hears from students, "I love Jesus, but hate the church.") Not only are evangelistic efforts within this population crucial to the survival of Christianity, but young people are also ripe for new presentations of the gospel message.
- **Those with Disabilities.** Most of our church buildings are not even accessible to those with disabilities, let alone equipped with aids for those who are visually or hearing impaired. It is not a surprise that a recent survey of people with disabilities indicated that the vast majority of them did not attend church since they felt they were not welcome there.
- **Sexual Minorities.** The full inclusion of LGBT people has been a major—some would say an all-consuming—topic

for many Christian churches over the last decade. Although much progress has been made, most LGBT people feel alienated from the church. It is said that one of the leading reasons that young people generally reject the church is their perception (no doubt correct in many cases) that Christians are homophobic and judgmental.[21] Statistics from most Western countries also make it clear that the attitude of churchgoers toward LGBT people is seriously out of step with those who don't go to church.

- **Recent Immigrants.** In Western Europe, workers arriving from the Middle East are more likely to bring their religion, Islam, along with them. However, in the United States the immigrants who are the most problematic, and most ignored, by American congregations are those arriving from Mexico and Central America. The overwhelming percentage of this group is Roman Catholic, but only nominally so. Their participation in church life often does not extend much beyond baptisms, weddings, funerals, and ethnic celebrations associated with Our Lady of Guadalupe and the Day of the Dead. A significant group of these Hispanic immigrants have found a new home in evangelical and Pentecostal churches where their pastoral needs are taken seriously, yet the vast majority remains essentially unaffiliated. With the population of many cities and even states being predominantly Hispanic, there is tremendous potential for our church among these people, who tend to have more children, be more family oriented, and, once they are members, more likely to attend church on a given Sunday than their Anglo counterparts. Many, including myself, are convinced that the Episcopal Church is ideally positioned to work with Hispanic people, offering them a church that combines a familiar sacramental approach with an emphasis on pastoral care. This is especially attractive to young Latina women, who are less willing to put up with a Roman Catholic hierarchy they perceive as having no particular concern for them or their spiritual needs.

We may remember too that the Church of England has a proven track record for mission work among those people "on the fringes," especially in Africa. It was there, from the late seventeenth century to the early twentieth century, that missionary societies such as the Society for the Propagation of the Gospel in Foreign Parts (SPG), the Church Missionary Society (CMS), and others laid the foundation for indigenous African ministries. Some of those churches are now the fastest growing in the world, far outpacing their parent bodies. It may come as a surprise, but there are far more Anglicans in Nigeria than there are in England!

The church is always at its best when it is looking outward. This is as true for individual congregations as it is for dioceses and denominations. Archbishop William Temple reminded us that the "church which lives for itself, dies by itself." That is why mission has always been the lifeblood of the church. Those populations who were "targets" for mission in turn became centers of vitality and expansion, and in turn raised up a new generation of missionaries. Pope Gregory could never have imagined that Anglo-Saxons, living in what was regarded as one of the furthest outposts of human settlement, would hundreds of years later bring the Christian message to millions living in "darkest Africa." Mission begets mission.

A CHURCH FOCUSED ON MISSION REQUIRES THE ABILITY TO ADAPT

A willingness to learn from indigenous cultures is perhaps the hardest task for missionaries. Nineteenth-century English missionaries in Africa and Indian are often castigated for being cultural chauvinists, more concerned with making their converts wear pants, have only one wife, and speak the King's English than they were with teaching the basics of the faith. A similar experience happened with Roman Catholic missionary efforts to Asia in the sixteenth century, where a rigid rejection of native practices and insistence on European standards, such as the Latin Mass, resulted in the failure of Christianity to greatly spread there.

One barometer of ecclesiastical inflexibility has been the reluctance of most churches to have indigenous clergy. Despite Church of England successes in Africa, there were no native-born priests in place until the middle of the nineteenth century, and there was no African bishop until

Samuel Crowther in 1857. In the United States the record is not much better. Alexander Crummell became the first black priest in 1844 (Absalom Jones had been ordained earlier but left the Episcopal Church) and John Burgess of Massachusetts was the first black elected diocesan bishop only in 1969.

When we turn to the example of the Augustinian mission, we have a mixed record. Clearly Gregory understood the need for flexibility better than Augustine did. In fact, Gregory's answers to Augustine regarding the existing pagan customs Augustine ought to simply incorporate into his own teaching reads like a textbook for missionary flexibility (for example, don't destroy pagan shrines if you can build a church on the site). This lesson, however, seems to have been lost on Augustine. As previously mentioned, in the famous meeting reported by Bede, Augustine rudely insulted a delegation of Celtic churchmen by refusing to rise to greet them. It is not clear whether this insult was intentional or inadvertent, but Bede's inclusion of the incident makes it clear that it was a notable setback to Augustine's future work, which would have been helped considerably by a good relationship with the bishops from Scotland and the north of England. The tension that was fueled by Augustine's lack of manners was not really resolved until almost a hundred years later at the Synod of Whitby (663).

The oldest book in England reminds us that bringing the gospel to people outside the recognized boundaries of the established church is more than a simple one-sided shout-out of the Good News. It involves listening and understanding the cultures we must reach, learning to "speak the language" of those whom we hope to reach. The church must do more listening and less talking if it hopes to reach people with its message.

Of course, any missionary initiative requires organization and structure. Gregory had at his disposal a cadre of trained and educated monks who knew their message and could rely upon one another for support and fellowship under difficult conditions. Yet they were able to adapt their monastic community life, formed in the heart of the Roman Church, to a very different environment where the culture, language, and religion was completely alien to the world they had left behind in Rome. From all indications, they made the transition enthusiastically.

In our church today we have all the resources we need to create a church for the future. It remains to be seen if we have the courage and flexibility to adapt to a new cultural environment. So far the signs are not encouraging. Just one example: My diocese has funding available to hire a new ordained priest to start an experimental chaplaincy at a new university. Although the position if fully funded and is a full-time job, it has proved enormously difficult to find a young priest who wants to take it on. Many candidates spoke passionately about "emergent church," but when it comes to deployment, an established curacy in a comfortable suburban setting is what everyone seems to be looking for.

St. Augustine's mission to England eventually resulted in a new synthesis of Roman learning and Anglo-Saxon culture. Within months of arriving, Pope Gregory was advising him to adapt Roman practices to local circumstances. And even though the Roman standard of doctrine and liturgy would not be formally adopted until the Synod of Whitby, it wasn't long before indigenous expressions of Christianity began to make themselves felt, not the least of which are the volumes of Anglo-Saxon sermons and texts made available to the local population.

So it will be in the church of the future. As the archbishop's Report on Mission so famously states, the church of the future will be a "mixed economy" with traditional forms of liturgy, worship, architecture, and governance coexisting with very untraditional and experimental "fresh expressions" of the faith.[22] I look forward to the time when members of our church can find near them a variety of choices on a given Sunday morning—Anglo-Catholic solemn High Mass, praise-band suburban family churches, liturgy in several different languages (especially Spanish), Christian Rap music, Taizé hymns, gothic-style naves, and house churches. Indeed in many places in the Anglican Communion, they already can. Above all, I look forward to a church that understands its very identity to be missional and where as much effort and money is spent reaching the unchurched as is spent meeting the pastoral needs of its current members, perhaps even more—a church where the faithful are as passionate about how they share the Good

News with those they meet every day as they are about what happens on Sunday morning.

David Bosch, in his magisterial work on the theology and history of Christian mission, points out that there is not just one style of mission, and that over the centuries the assumptions and techniques of evangelization have changed. But one thing remains the same, the fact that "mission is not a function of the church, it is the fundamental expression of its life."[23] This is why it is important for us in the modern church to be aware of what has gone before when it comes to Christian mission.

"We do not stand at the end of mission," but rather at the end of a specific period of mission history. "The harsh realities of today compel us to re-conceive and reformulate the church's mission, to do this boldly and imaginatively, yet also in continuity with the best of what mission has been in past decades and centuries."[24]

These themes were echoed in our former presiding bishop's sermon to the 2009 General Convention when she concluded, "There is a heartbeat of the church. . . . If you listen you can hear it—it's called mission, mission, mission."[25]

The "Five Marks of Mission" ratified at the Lambeth Conference of 2008 are likely to serve as a litmus test for evaluating church structures in a time of great economic stress. Those programs, boards, and agencies that do not meet the criteria of the Five Marks are likely to find themselves out of business.

— II —

Manuscript

I walked into the Porter's Lodge of Corpus Christi College in Cambridge on a bright summer morning in 2012 with butterflies in my stomach. I had come a long way to revisit this book, which I had seen briefly while attending the Lambeth Conference in 2008. Then, I had touched it for only a few minutes. Now I planned to spend three days with it. I identified myself to the porter, who called the librarian, Christopher de Hamel. A few minutes later he came bounding into the room, as enthusiastic as I remembered him. "We have been expecting you," he cried. "The book has been expecting you!" Together we walked across the quadrangle to the entrance to the newly refurbished Parker Library.

In 2010 H.R.H. Prince Philip was on hand to dedicate this new facility. It is equipped with state of the art climate control and security, and contains the most valuable of the Parker Library holdings. Dr. de Hamel told me how he breathed a sigh of relief when ancient books and manuscripts were finally transported from their old homes on nineteenth-century, second-story bookshelves—where undergraduates were allowed to study unsupervised—to their new secure location below.

I was to learn later that Dr. de Hamel has made a point of making the collection of the Parker Library more accessible to the public. Indeed his excitement over his collection is contagious. At several points during my stay he would run out of his office with some rare treasure he wanted to share with me: "One of the earliest copies of the *Anglo-Saxon Chronicle,* mostly likely King Alfred's own!" he would say as he slid an ancient leather-bound tome under my nose. Perhaps Dr. de Hamel's passion for sharing comes from the fact that, as a graduate student, he was denied access to a manuscript in the Parker Library! "They didn't let anyone in in those days," he laments. All the more reason for making up for it now.

I was introduced to the assistant librarian, Gill Cannell, and assigned a place at a long reading table, equipped with a special foam rubber stand to support the book. "Do I need to wear gloves?" I asked. "No, just be careful. It is, after all, the oldest book in England," I was reminded. Dr. de Hamel disappeared into the inner vault and a few minutes later returned with a large wooden book. "I will leave you two alone," he quipped, and bounded off to other business. I opened the box, gently took out a heavy volume bound in oak boards and white fabric, and placed it on the reading stand. My time with Augustine's relic, his own Gospel book, was about to begin.

Corpus Christi College Manuscript 286 (from now on I'll simply call it MS 286) consists of 265 leaves or *folia* written on a very fine parchment, possibly goatskin rather than the usual sheepskin. The text of the four Gospels is of course in Latin written in a good hand (one scholar detects evidence of five separate scribes). The style of writing or font itself is called *uncial* (literally "inch-high letters") and is remarkably clear and easy for a modern reader to follow. It is especially important to note that this style of uncial writing was the script of late antiquity associated with Rome. Indeed, during the medieval period uncial writing was called *littera romana*, Roman letters. Augustine and his monks were Romans, and so was the alphabet they read.[1]

The page layout itself follows the practice first employed by St. Jerome in his fifth-century Vulgate translation of the Bible, which grouped the text into short paragraphs or sections (*per cola et commata*). Over the ages, the parchment has taken on a light brown patina, and the ink is no longer black (except where later annotations have been made) and reminded me of the color of cappuccino. Most pages of the text are intact, but, sadly, all but two of the pictures have disappeared. What remains is a portrait of St. Luke the Evangelist and a page containing twelve small scenes from the life of Jesus. There were originally more illuminated pages, following the same pattern for the other three Evangelists. Indeed traces of the ink from these are still visible on the pages that originally faced them. The MS may also have contained a decorated Eusebian canons page, common to all Gospel books of the time. In the days before the Bible was divided up into chapter and verse—a practice introduced in early printed Bibles of the sixteenth century—the Eusebian canons provided a way of cross-referencing the four Gospel books. Readers could consult this table, in which the four Gospel books were compared and agreement noted.

It is of special note that MS 286 is bound with several early Anglo-Saxon charters dating from the tenth and eleventh centuries. This was a common practice of that time, akin to our grandparents' use of the "family Bible" as a repository for birth records and other vital information. To inscribe the text of a land agreement or charitable donation in the pages of a Bible manuscript was a way of insuring its sacred and permanent character. There is also an interesting bit of literary graffiti on one of the end flyleaves. Count Constantin von Tischendorf, famous for his discovery (and virtual theft) of the Codex Sinaiticus from St. Catherine's monastery in 1859—arguably the most important ancient

Bible text in the world—examined MS 286 in 1842. Von Tischendorf was in England that year in his quest to find the most ancient New Testament texts and left his signature and comments on the vellum of MS 286 to prove it.

Where was this manuscript made, and how did it get to its current home? Thanks to the efforts of generations of scholars, we now have relatively reliable answers to those questions.

From its style of penmanship, we know that the manuscript was composed in Rome in the late sixth century. It is doubtful that it was intended to be a deluxe "presentation copy." One scholar comments that its "parchment and [page] patching indicate either an inferior production center or a product intended for an inferior region."[2] Still, we should remember that the making of any medieval book was a time-consuming and costly venture. It is pure speculation on my part, but I like to think that our MS was an "extra" Gospel book from the library of St. Andrew's Monastery in Rome, the same monastery Pope Gregory had founded upon his own ancestral villa on the Caelian Hill and where Augustine had been a monk until chosen by Gregory for the journey to England. Carrying part of one's spiritual heritage to a new mission field would have been an understandable and appropriate gesture.

The artwork is another indication of its origin. One wishes that more of the illuminated miniatures had survived—they were most likely cut out at the time of the dissolution of the monastic library at Canterbury during the

English Reformation. What remains of the artwork points to the influence of classical models available in Rome at the time. The figure of St. Luke, for example, is in keeping with portrayals of Roman emperors and ancient philosophers. The art historian Francis Wormald has assembled pictures of some of these ancient exemplars, and the similarities to the figure of St. Luke in our manuscript are striking. Whoever drew the pictures that have come down to us in the St. Augustine Gospels was a keen observer of the statues and images on display in the Rome in that day.

Just as ancient art served as a model for MS 286, our manuscript in turn had a marked impact on future artistic work. Several later Gospel books are clearly based upon it, some quite well known in paleographic circles (paleography is the study of ancient writing), such as the Codex Aureus ("Golden Book"—so called because it contains the first illustrations to be decorated with gold leaf), now in the Stockholm Kungliga Biblioteket (Cod. A.135). At least two famous surviving Gospel books dating from a slightly later period also display a reliance on the St. Augustine Gospels even though they were produced in Italy: the Codex Oxoniensis (Bodleian Library, MS Auct. D. 214 [2698]) and the Harley Gospels (British Library, Harley MS 1775).

Doubtless our manuscript was well studied by scribes through the southern part of England. Mildred Budny, in her lengthy study of Anglo-Saxon art, believes that the manuscript's illustrations also served as models for stained-glass windows in Canterbury Cathedral hundreds of years later, and perhaps even exercised an influence on the Bayeux tapestry, which Budny believes was stitched in or near Canterbury.[3]

The manuscript remained in Canterbury for most of its history. It was considered such a treasure that it was kept in the treasury of the Augustine's abbey just outside the walls of the city. Because of its association with the person of St. Augustine, it was from the start treated more as a relic than a book. It was during its stay in Canterbury that Anglo-Saxon and later Latin charters, covering a period from 989 to 1224, were bound with it. These charters document dealings the abbots had with local landowners, and it was vital that those documents be saved and protected.

There is considerable consensus that the manuscript came with Augustine when he landed on the Isle of Thanet in 597, although it is also possible that it found its way there a few years later in 601, when Augustine's assistant Mellitus arrived with further supplies from Rome. According to Bede, he brought with him "all such things as were necessary for the worship and ministry of the church . . . [including] very many books [*codices plurimos*]."[4] I've opted for the earlier date since surely a copy of the Gospels would have been essential equipment for preaching, celebrating the Mass, and teaching. Augustine would not have been able to function without it or some other books that gained a reputation of having arrived with him.

We can speculate what some of these books were: a Bible, most likely written in more than one volume; a psalter; and very possibility a copy of Gregory's treatise, *Pastoral*

Care. Apparently these books were venerated from the earliest foundation of the monastery at Canterbury, although thanks to the analysis of modern scholars, it appears that some of the books associated with Augustine are from a later date than that of MS 286.

These volumes have the special distinction of being portrayed by a medieval artist. An illustration found in a late medieval manuscript likely shows the Gospels along with several other venerated volumes lying upon the altar during High Mass in the abbey. Thomas of Elmham, a monk at the Abbey from 1374 to 1418, in his *Speculum Augustinianum* (Trinity Hall MS 1—1417), listed eight books in the abbey's collection as associated with St. Augustine and Pope Gregory: "*primitivae librorum totius ecclesiae Anglicanae*—the earliest of the books of the whole English church."[5] A full-page drawing in color shows six of them resting on the high altar. Below them is the label "*libri missi a Gregorio ad Augustinum* [books sent by Gregory to Augustine]." Two are labeled as Gospel books. These same books are also mentioned briefly by two earlier monks, Thomas Sprott in 1270 and William Thorne in 1370, as books which "*Gregorius misit ad beatum Augustinum* [books Gregory sent to blessed Augustine]."[6] Although this is not conclusive evidence, it indicates that the authenticity of our MS was unquestioned by its medieval owners. There is further evidence that during its time at the abbey, it was venerated for its close connection with its founder. It is not mentioned in an inventory of the abbey library made in the fourteenth century, probably due to the fact that it resided in the treasury rather than the library. The fact that it does not contain a library pressmark also supports this assumption. In short, it was considered more of a relic than a book, which makes its survival even more remarkable when the monastic community at Canterbury was dissolved and its contents were scattered by order of Thomas Cromwell in 1538, since the reformers had little tolerance for relics and their cultic veneration.

Here occurs an apparent lacuna in tracing the provenance of MS 286. During the general chaos that prevailed during the dissolution and closing of the monasteries during the time of the English Reformation in the sixteenth century, many valuable manuscripts were lost, misplaced, or simply burned. Some scholars and book collectors, like the antiquarian John Bale, did their best to rescue books that were thought to have historical value. In a letter to the archbishop of Canterbury, Matthew Parker, dated July 30, 1560, and signed, Bale vividly describes the obstacles he faced in acquiring and transporting such books:

> [These books] I obtayned in tyme of the lamentable spoule of the lybrayers of Englande, through much fryndshypp, labour and expenses. Some I founde in stacyoners and boke bynders store howses, some in grosers, sopesellars, taylers, and other ocurpyers shoppes, some in shyppes ready to be carryed over the sea

into Flanders to be solde. For in those uncircumspect and careless dayes, there was no quyckar merschaundyce than lybrary bokes, and all to the destructuon of learnyning and knowledge of thynges necessary in thys fall of Antichriste to be knowne, but the Devyll is a knave, they say.[7]

It may be that Archbishop Parker acquired MS 286 from Bale or one of his fellow antiquaries, although this is really anyone's guess. It is interesting to note that over one hundred Abbey manuscripts survived the destruction and may have been "inherited" by Archbishop Parker when he assumed his office in 1559.

We will pick up the story of the archbishop's involvement with MS 286 in section four of this book. Suffice it to say for now that Parker may not have known what he had. He was probably far more interested in the Anglo-Saxon charters bound with the Gospels. As for the Latin text, he seems to have believed that he was in possession of a Gospel book that had belonged to Archbishop Theodore of Tarsus, who succeeded Augustine as the seventh archbishop of Canterbury from 668–690.

In any event, Parker brought the manuscript to Cambridge, where it has been ever since. Archbishop Parker entrusted it to his alma mater, Corpus Christi College, a year before his death in 1575. Along with about 500 manuscripts and many printed books, it formed the core of the Parker Library, which has been keep intact ever since.

The manuscript was examined and described by several later catalogers: Thomas James (1600), William Stanley (1722), James Nasmith (1777), and Montague Rhodes James (1909–1912). In addition, there is a catalog of the manuscripts in French by Nigel Wilkins (1993) and a catalog of the decorated manuscripts up to c. 1100 by Mildred Budny (1997). It was rebound in 1748 and again in 1949. Since 1945, it has been the Gospel book upon which every new archbishop of Canterbury has sworn his oath of office. It was present at the joint prayer service at Canterbury Cathedral with Archbishop Robert Runcie and Pope John Paul II, and most recently at Pope Benedict XVI's visit to Westminster Abbey in 2010. As of this writing, it has not left English soil for 1,415 years.

— III —

Communication

"May we see the magic book again, Father Augustine?" This was the third time this week that Aelfwald and his young friend had appeared at the monastery door. It was a nuisance to have to stop his correspondence, get up from the writing desk, and fetch the book down from its locked shelf, but Augustine resignedly did so. After all, he could hardly blame his new flock for their curiosity about the book and its pictures. He was still incredulous that they had never seen any. These Saxon folk had metalwork that was easily the equal to anything found in Rome, he thought, but when it came to paintings and drawings they had none. He carefully opened the Gospel book on the desk, with the two boys pressed up against him on either side to get a good look. They were not interested in the beautiful Latin writing that had taken some poor scribe in Rome so long to do. No, they wanted him instead to turn to the pictures of the Gospel writers surrounded by animals and scenes from Jesus's life. Augustine knew that once he had their attention, they would listen for hours as he described the pictures. "This is Jesus," he said, pointing to a small colorful miniature of Christ surrounded by his disciples. "It is the *cena domini*, the last supper that Jesus ate with his friends. When you are baptized, you can eat this holy meal with Jesus too." The boys gazed at him wide-eyed. Augustine once again thought of the wisdom of his friend and master Pope Gregory. How right he had been to give him this book with its many pictures before he left Rome. The old saying, "a picture is worth a thousand words," was certainly true. Even more true, a picture purchased the souls of many new converts.

How would the manuscript we know as the St. Augustine Gospels have been used? Who would have seen it? What impact did it have on its viewers?

Binding the four Gospels of Matthew, Mark, Luke, and John into one volume made them available for liturgical reading during the Mass. In the ancient church, as in liturgical churches today, a volume containing the four Gospels, often ornately decorated, is carried by a deacon or priest into the midst of the congregation where a designated portion is read out loud according to a table of readings known as the lectionary. The book itself is venerated as a sacred object, symbolizing Christ's presence in the congregation through the written word. It is carried in procession, accompanied by candles, and "censed" before it is held up to been seen by all before and after it is read. Church practice requires that at every celebration of the Holy Eucharist a portion of the Gospels be read publicly. Since these Gospel books have a specific function to play, they have to be designed accordingly. Not only are they impressive in appearance, sometimes with elaborate bindings of precious metal and jewels, but the text itself has to be of such a size that it can be read when an acolyte holds the book open at arm's length from the reader. Throughout the medieval period, the four Gospels were bound with an ancient reference guide known as the Eusebian canons, which allowed the reader to cross-reference a given Gospel passage with similar accounts in the other Gospels. They were also usually bound with a letter from St. Jerome regarding the authority and order of the four books. Our manuscript most likely once contained these items, although they are now missing.

What our manuscript does contain that makes it unusual are illustrations (in medieval documents known as "illuminations"), even though most of them were at some point cut out of the book, perhaps at the time of the Reformation. As some of the earliest manuscript illuminations in existence, those that survive are extremely important for the student of art history. Why were these illuminations included when they are too small to be seen by anyone except the public reader of the book? Why go to so much trouble, when the text alone would suffice? MS 286 is not unique in this regard. Gospel collections that date not much later also contain illustrations, and as time went on, this pictoral work became larger and more ornate, culminating in the almost baroque displays of "insular" or Celtic-style calligraphy such as are seen in the Lindisfarne Gospels (c. 700) or the Book of Kells (c. 800). There are at least four reasons that scribes would have labored so hard to produce works of art like the St. Augustine Gospels:

1. *The natural and common human impulse to decorate objects that are holy or special to us.* The impulse toward decoration is shared by all cultures. We ornament that which we value.

2. *The spiritual benefit that comes from undertaking such work.* Sacred art is done "for the glory of God alone," whether anyone is going to see that work or not. We know that this was the case, for example, with the Lindisfarne Gospels, which were undertaken by its illustrator Bishop Eadfrith, "as a heroic one man feat of prayer and praise," according to historian Michelle Brown.[1]

3. *To enhance the supernatural value of a sacred object.* This imperative is still with us as believers to decorate churches with liturgical art, enclose objects associated with saints in jeweled reliquaries, or venerate icon

paintings as "windows" into heaven. We know that when Augustine landed on the Isle of Thanet off the Kentish coast, he carried with him a painting (icon?) of Jesus along with a silver processional cross. Bede makes a point of mentioning these. We can imagine the impact that this object must have had on a culture that had never before seen a pictorial image in any form! The illustrations in our MS 286 must have had a similar, although perhaps less public, effect. Christopher de Hamel comments, "It was evidently very important that right from the onset the monks should exhibit a visual image of the new religion which could have been seen and wondered over even before they began explaining the message of Scripture." That the "medium is the message" was especially true of books, which made it vital for the missionaries to have books—to read from, to carry publicly, and to display pictures. "Christianity is the religion of the book and its message goes with literacy, a concept new to many of its British converts," de Hamel continues. "Missionaries, then and now, could face skeptical audiences with the Gospels under their arms—a specific manual for salvation in debate against a religion based on oral tradition—and the scarcely literate are quite rightly impressed by the written word."[2]

4. *To use for instructional purposes.* Pope Gregory himself commented to Bishop Serenus of Marseilles around 600, "In images the illiterate read."

It is this last reason that is the most important for us here. We can be sure that when Augustine's Gospel book was not serving in its sacramental role in worship, it was examined, studied, and even copied by people who saw it. It certainly did not gather dust on the shelf of the sacristy! As mentioned before, art historians have detected its influence in much of the manuscript illustration that took place in England during the next two hundred years or so. Thus the St. Augustine Gospels is not only the "oldest book in England," but also the oldest example of biblical manuscript illumination in Western Europe.

Of special note are the four folio pages—of which only one survives—containing twelve scenes from Jesus's life. They accompanied larger portraits of the four Evangelists with their respective symbolic animals. There would originally have been forty-eight of these "thumbnails" of the life and ministry of Christ. We have the page that goes with St. Luke; if that one is any clue, each of the other three pages emphasized events important to that respective evangelist.

Here are the scenes on the Luke folio (on page 65), in the order in which they are portrayed:

The Annunciation to Mary	Jesus teaching the crowd
Boy Jesus in the temple	Jesus conversing with a woman
Preaching from a boat	Jesus conversing with the
The calling of Peter	crowd
A dead man raised	Cursing the fig tree
Jesus speaking with a man	Jesus with a beggar
	Calling Zacchaeus

The Evangelist St. Luke surrounded by scenes from Jesus's life. The figure of the Gospel writer bears a strong resemblance to contemporary statues of Roman philosophers. Corpus Christi College, MS 286, f.129v.

Scenes from the passion of Jesus. The image of Jesus at the last supper in the top center panel is the oldest portrayal of this event in any ancient manuscript. Jesus appears as a clean-shaven Roman youth. Corpus Christi College, MS 286, f125r.

Even more dramatic and colorful is the other surviving illustration (on page 66), which contains larger thumbnails of scenes of the passion of Jesus, all centered on the scene of the Last Supper at the top and center of the page:

Entry into Jerusalem	Before the high priest
Raising of Lazarus	Led to Golgotha
Arrest in the garden	Garden of Gethsemane
Pilate sentences Jesus	Judas's betrayal
Last Supper	Jesus mocked
Washing disciples' feet	Carrying cross

Would any of these have had a special resonance with Augustine's Anglo-Saxon audience? Probably not. This is another reason we can conclude that the manuscript was not produced especially for Augustine to take with him on his English mission, but was simply an already available codex. Yet it is important to note the centrality of the portrayal of the *cena domini* at the top center of the folio, for it is the oldest pictorial representation of the Eucharist in any manuscript in existence. It is striking in its simplicity and directness. Notice that Jesus is portrayed as clean-shaven, as a Roman youth of the sixth century would have been, not as a hirsute barbarian (the word comes from the same root word as "beard" and "barber"). This might have required a certain amount of explaining to Anglo-Saxon viewers for whom a full beard was a sign of masculine power and virility!

In a dramatic way, the book that St. Augustine brought with him to England marked a turning point in the use of media technology for his new converts. It is not hard to imagine the impact that seeing an image of Jesus must have made on them. It must have seemed truly magical that they could also *see* as well as *hear* about the central figure of their new religion. No wonder Aethelbert feared Augustine's magical powers! As happens when any technologically advanced culture encounters a more primitive one, it is the technology itself that contributes to conquest of one people by another. This would later be the case when South American native peoples were visited by horse-mounted Spanish conquistadores in the sixteenth century, and when Native Americans experienced the guns and cannons of white settlers in the seventeenth century. The impression that Augustine and his band of monks must have made with their ability to read from books and to paint pictures of what they had seen was a skill more peaceful but no less powerful. It was the first step in turning an oral culture into a written culture. Those who controlled the communication medium would henceforth control the country. For the Anglo-Saxons, it was more than just a religious conversion, it was the beginning of a social revolution.

We too live in a time of great technological revolution: in our case, the dawn of the digital age. It now goes without saying that the advances made in Internet technology and communications have had a profound impact on our lives. Any communications expert would agree that computer-based communication has had more impact on the way that we process information, spend our free time, run our businesses, and relate to each other than any other technological shift in human history. Far more than, say, the impact of the printing press in the sixteenth century following the invention of moveable type by Johannes Gutenberg in 1455.

The digital encyclopedia Wikipedia provides a good definition of this technological seismic shift:

> The Digital Revolution known as the **Third Industrial Revolution** is the change from analog, mechanical, and electronic technology to digital technology which began anywhere from the late 1950s to the late 1970s with the adoption and proliferation of digital computers and digital record keeping that continues to the present day. Implicitly, the term also refers to the sweeping changes brought about by digital computing and communication technology during (and after) the latter half of the 20th century. Analogous to the Agricultural Revolution and Industrial Revolution, the Digital Revolution marked the beginning of the Information Age.[3]

There are many examples of the shift from analog to digital: We once listened to music on LP records, then on CDs, then mp3s, and now there are streaming services on the Internet or our phones; films have moved from the theater, to tape, to disc, and now they too stream over the Internet; digital technology has made watching television on an HDTV an entirely different experience than it was on an analog set connected to an antenna. We once had to ask an operator to connect us to another person's telephone, but now we can talk to them on our cell phones by touching his or her name. The examples are endless, and there are many things we do today that have little correspondence with the analog age, such as social media and texting. There is a mountain of literature on the impact the digital age has had, and continues to have, on our political, economic, and social lives. As in the case of all technologies, the medium is itself neutral—neither inherently good nor bad—even though it brings with it both positive and negative consequences.

Among the positive effects of digital communication are greater interconnectedness and ease of communication. Most of us use the web to keep in touch with friends, family, and business clients, and if you are like the majority of Americans, you have also used it to reconnect with a long-lost family member or nearly forgotten school friend. This interconnectivity also results in a democratization of information. No longer can totalitarian regimes restrict the flow of news and criticism of their governments, and the results have been dramatic, such as the role Twitter played in the 2010 "Arab Spring." The Internet has reshaped the economic world as well by allowing for global outsourcing, as when you call your credit card company to get information on your account and find yourself speaking to someone in India! Thanks to the web, small regional companies can now market worldwide. As for workers, it is generally agreed that use of web technology markedly increases productivity, even with the temptation for employees to waste time with personal e-mail, playing FarmVille, or checking Facebook.

On the downside, the negative effects of connectivity include information overload, Internet predators, and forms of social isolation (it's true—you *can* do your work, watch your favorite movies, and order all your food without ever leaving your computer screen!). Connectivity also leads to invasions of privacy: Some companies track online activity and tailor their advertising to our personal preferences, and some employers monitor the number of keystrokes an employee makes at their computer each day. If you would like a more complete list of pros and cons of social media, there is even a website for that: socialnetworking.procon.org!

What is germane to this study is how the digital revolution has impacted the institutional church, and what opportunities it presents for the future of Christianity. It is my belief that there is much we can learn from the experience of Augustine's mission, especially in his use of visual art to impress his potential converts. Manuscript 286 provides us an early object lesson in the use of media technology.

Fortunately there has been much work on the religious role of digital media. Elizabeth Drescher has written two books on the topic: *Tweet If You [Heart] Jesus* and

Click 2 Save.[4] She begins by giving the reader a summary of how the church has in the past both used and, more often, ignored technology in communicating its message. She refers to an interview I had with her several years ago in which I said, "[The church] blew it with radio; we blew it with television. The question is whether we'll be able to make use of these new tools while there is still a window of opportunity."[5]

She reminds us of the very funny viral video that made the rounds a few years ago. In what was originally a TV skit for Norwegian Television, an older monk is introduced to the use of a new medieval technology—the book! He just can't get the hang of it, and has to have the help of a younger and more "tech-savvy" brother to instruct him in such basic operating procedures as opening the cover, page turning, etc. Like all good satire, the skit pokes fun at our often clueless attempts to come to grips with new electronic gizmos and computer operating systems that increasingly dominate our lives. And like most satire, it would be funnier if it were not so true.[6]

A workshop I attended not long ago with several of my fellow bishops was intended to help us communicate more effectively when interviewed on television. The leader had just stated how important it was to be knowledgeable about communications technology when one bishop raised his hand to ask, "Yes, I hear people talking about blogging— what exactly is a blog, anyway?" I further recall a lunchtime conversation with the senior warden of a congregation in the Diocese of Arizona who said to me: "I take pride in the fact I've never touched a computer and never will—as far as I am concerned, that stuff is for kids." It was all I could do from asking, "Should we just close the doors of your church now, or wait until next year?"

For the most part, the church has missed the opportunities technology offered it to reach people with the gospel message. A case in point is its reluctance to use Facebook and Twitter, two of the best free gifts God has given the church! Even though a large percentage of our parishioners use these outlets on a regular basis, there are only a handful of congregations that make use of them through daily or even weekly postings. In the House of Bishops in the Episcopal Church, my recent estimate is that although about a third of the bishops have a Twitter account, only about fifteen or twenty (out of 110 active bishops) use them regularly and effectively.

That is why Drescher wants to move beyond cataloging our past failures and challenge the church to seize the opportunities we are presented with. It should be pointed out that many churches have already done so. In a recent segment of the PBS show *Religion and Ethics*,[7] several examples were given. One megachurch reaches over a third of its Sunday audience via electronic connection. Another pastor speaks of how he has replaced a simple "I will pray for you" with an e-mail follow-up with his parishioners. A house church has formed around a big-screen TV, originally purchased to watch sports, until "God had another idea." There is even an order of Roman Catholic nuns, the Order of the Daughters of Saint Paul, who have dedicated themselves to using the Internet to reach potential converts. Sister Susan James Heady says, "Whereas maybe people before might have thought they had to go to church to do religion, now they are doing it in the comfort of their home, having religious and theological discussions with their friends—maybe even a lot more fun because people like to get on their computer and go on Facebook."

The shift is not without its challenges for established churches. Professor Stephen O'Leary, of the Annenberg School for Communication at the University of Southern California, says on the *Religion and Ethics* episode: "In many cases, members of the congregation are acting as media producers and are functioning independently of their own local church. So the authorities from the church— pastor up the line to the denominational heads—no longer have the kind of control that they once did."[8] This includes the control of information. Sister Susan James adds, "When we have a question about theology we can't answer, we have Scripture, but we also have Google!" No longer does a believer need to go to church to have their religious questions answered. The Internet is a limitless— though not always accurate—source of information, available 24/7.

Even these tech-savvy leaders are quick to add that technology is just one tool, albeit a very powerful one, in the service of God's kingdom, even though no one would go so far as to substitute a computer for face-to-face communication. In an article on this subject in *USA Today*, Eugene Sutton, bishop of the Episcopal Diocese of Maryland, is quoted, "In the search for personal spiritual fulfillment, nothing can replace the joy and lasting value of sharing one's faith journey in person with another human being."[9] Yet when asked if they would go back to a traditional kind of church, most members of these new digital faith communities answer, "Probably not."

Still, digital church communities like these are the exception, not the rule. The church secretary in most congregations now uses e-mail as matter of course, and a forward-thinking priest might use Facebook to keep in contact with parishioners or post his sermons on a blog, but most congregations and church organizations are woefully behind when it comes to using social media. A recent study indicated that only 20 percent of Episcopal churches have an active website, and of those, most contain inaccurate or out-of-date information. When 97 percent of American businesses state that their social media presence is their number one concern—and with 75 percent of those planning to spend more money on social media this year than last—one wonders what church leaders can possibly be thinking?[10]

Elizabeth Drescher sums up:

> It seems clearer and clearer that the ever-growing dominance of social media—especially on mobile computing devices like smartphones and tablets—is bringing religion back into the daily lives of many, while challenging religious institutions to revise notions of spiritual identity and community in both online and face-to-face worship. . . .
>
> More than new gimmicks for those who already love religion, these new digitally influenced practices have the potential to move those who love social media as well as those who dig a good brew or a healthy hike to re-engage with traditions that have for too long excluded them by functioning only outside of their everyday experience. They hold out the possibility to reboot faith communities that have long been flashing "fail" to believers and seekers alike.[11]

As in Augustine's time, the church must embrace and welcome new forms of communication. As an institution, we lag behind every group when it comes to use of new technology. This is especially true of those of us who as Episcopalians are part of what used to be called "mainline" churches. While megachurch leaders find ways to simulcast their worship services to remote locations, some of our smaller churches still don't even have an e-mail address. An old joke is that "fundamentalists can build atomic weapons, but we can't even get the PA system to work." I find this technological backwardness puzzling, in that most folks in our congregations are using the Internet in their daily lives, but there is a disconnect when it comes to its use in church. An excuse I often hear is "we have many elderly people in our congregation, and they don't know about computers." Tell that to my ninety-two-year-old parents, who treasure their iPad and love to Skype with their grandkids! I would venture to say that much of the resistance to using technology in the church comes not from the members but from the leadership, especially the clergy, who see it not as a technological challenge but as another drain on their time. No one likes to spend the time to learn something new, but it is sad for me that they cannot see how judicious use of digital media could increase their productivity (and thus save time). More importantly, many don't see how it can help them reach both the churched and unchurched in exciting ways.

So where might our clergy and congregations get started?

Digital Technology Is Accessible

You don't have to be an expert, and there are plenty of people in your congregation who are willing and able to help bring you and your church into the twenty-first century. Many of these folks are young. Unlike those of us who are older, they don't see the Internet as a toy or novelty but as an essential part of life. Here is yet another place where we old-timers can learn from them.

START WITH THE BASICS: E-MAIL

If your church still doesn't have an e-mail account, get one
and use it. They are free or very low cost. Although e-mail is
now considered "old school," it still has its important uses:

- An e-mail newsletter will reach a wider audience than
  will print, while saving postage costs. Many parishes and
  dioceses now use e-mail exclusively, although for such
  "print media" types as Episcopalians, it probably still
  pays to have an occasional "snail mail" newsletter.
- E-mail can instantly update your congregation with
  late-breaking news as well as reminders about upcoming events. Once a listserv is set up, a press of a button can let your congregation know of the funeral of a
  long-time parishioner, the cancellation of a service due
  to bad weather, or the need for more potato salad at the
  parish picnic.
- E-mailed columns from a bishop or priest to the congregation have the effect of strengthening that relationship
  (this is also true of Facebook and Twitter, see below).
  When I was a parish priest, I wrote a monthly column
  called "Rector.com." Not the best name, to be sure, but
  people got the point and by the time I left that parish,
  my mailing list was several hundred people who actually
  looked forward to hearing what I had to say each week.
  In the early days of this medium, there was no provision for them to comment or offer feedback, and as we

will see, it is this interactive dimension of social media that makes it so powerful. When I got to be bishop, my weekly column morphed into "E-pistle," but the content was similar; like a newspaper columnist I not only had the chance to share my thinking but to respond in a very quick way to events in the life of a parish, something I could never do with the long lead time required to print and mail a hard copy.

- Using e-mail for prayers is something I am just learn-ing. A clergy friend I know told me, "I used to just say to members of my flock who were in need, 'I will pray for you,' a good response but it didn't have much depth. Now I write them an e-mail and include the words of my prayer for them. Many recipients tell me they carry that prayer with them and take strength from it during the day." Here is a good example of how a medium that many consider shallow—not requiring as much thought as a well-crafted handwritten note—can in fact take someone to a much deeper spiritual place.

WEBSITES

When it comes to websites, simply having one is only part of the solution. Many congregations, especially smaller ones, assume that it is difficult and expensive to set up a website. Now about 70% of American churches have a functioning website, yet most are not current or effective and this is a sad statistic given the fact that 80 percent of people looking for a

church to attend go to the web to find one![12] Is there any business or institution in this country today that does not have a
website? If your church does not have a website, it is easy to
create one. As an experiment, a group I belong to recently
created a website in about 45 minutes for a cost of $19.99.

The greater problem with church websites is they are
seldom used to their full potential. Even if the information posted online is up-to-date and current, the web page
often functions only as a kind of electronic bulletin board
for parishioners to check the summer service schedule or
whether the time of choir practice has been changed. What
is almost always lacking is content that would be interesting
to potential members. Every church website should have
answers to such questions as "What is the Episcopal Church?"
"What are our core values as a congregation?" "What might
I expect if I were to attend one of your services?"

One rapidly growing church I know of in Texas even
provides an online video of what it calls, "A Sunday morning test drive," where potential church visitors can see a
preview of what a typical Sunday morning worship service
looks like. In addition to service times, guests are also interested in more mundane questions like where to park and
what are the provisions for nursery care. I used to be skeptical about the practice of some clergy posting their latest
sermon online (in either video, audio, or written form).
This seemed a tad egocentric to me until a number of new
members told me that by reading the sermon they could tell
whether they would feel comfortable in attending.

It has been my experience that congregations need not worry so much about the aesthetic appearance or design of their website, as long as the information conveyed is helpful and up-to-date—the kind of site that regular parishioners will want to visit a least once a week, and newcomers will find helpful as an orientation. This means that churches need not budget for expensive web designers and artists. There is no need for revolving pictures and eye-catching visual effects. A simple way of getting regular parishioners to use the website is to post current pictures of them every week. Everyone likes to look at themselves, plus ever-changing shots of parishioners engaged in parish life will attract new members.

SOCIAL MEDIA

I am convinced that Facebook is God's greatest free gift to the church. The potential that this wonderful invention has for creating and strengthening existing social structures is almost limitless. From our laptops at home we have access to a major segment of the world's population—amazing! The world's largest "nations" are, by population, China, India, Facebook, the United States, Twitter, and Brazil. It is so disappointing that this unprecedented resource is so misunderstood and underused by most congregations. In my diocese, I only know of about fifteen out of sixty-five congregations that are making use of Facebook in any meaningful way. Surprisingly, two of these congregations are among the smallest (but fastest growing!) of our churches.

Perhaps the most effective example I know of a lever-aged use of Facebook is by our now-retired missioner to Native youth, Kaze Gadeway in Northern Arizona. Kaze not only uses Facebook to create community among her group of Spirit Youth, young Navajos who often do not have a permanent place to live or a home telephone (but they do have a smartphone!), but also, thanks to her daily posts and comments about her work, she has built a nationwide network of "Facebook friends" who support her prayerfully and financially. Among the ranks of those friends are a number of bishops and the former president of the House of Deputies! Kaze is not some geeky millennial—she is a former social worker in her late sixties who lives in a hogan at the end of dirt road with no electricity or running water. She often taps into a free wifi connection at the McDonalds in Holbrook, Arizona. She operates on less than a shoestring, yet thanks to Facebook she is able to involve her young people in a variety of learning experiences that are helping them become future leaders of the Native community. She is a model of the power of new technology to do the work of the kingdom of God.

Kaze's story is an example of the remarkable power that social media gives the church to share its story with the rest of the world. For almost no cost, Kaze has impacted the lives of thousands of people around the world, and she has saved the lives of some of her youth, many of whom are struggling with issues of addiction and abuse that are hard for the rest of us to imagine. It has been said that Facebook is "word of mouth on steroids," and that is true. More than just a way for church members to stay in touch and share their lives in words and pictures (the picture part of this equation is now being rapidly assumed by a platform Facebook has purchased—Instagram), it is also a powerful medium for sharing with others the Christian message, not through heavy-handed recruitment, but by simply letting one's Facebook friends know—"Went to church this morning and it was great!" Via social media, that message can be relayed and multiplied in ways we can hardly calculate, and reach people we hardly know.

It has long been known that a personal recommendation is the most effective means of getting someone to visit a church. All of us are in church because someone brought us there. A simple invitation—"I like the church I attend; it has a positive impact on my life. Would you like to come with me and check it out?"—is far more effective than TV or radio advertising, or direct mail, and certainly much cheaper! Imagine how many people could be reached if every parishioner in a medium-sized 200-member church went home on Sunday and reported to their Facebook friends (the average is between 200 and 500) that they had been to church: 200 x 500 = 10,000! This is why I often begin my sermon in the congregations I visit with these words: "I know that in many public places, you are asked to turn off your phones before the service begins. Well, I want to invite you to turn them on!"

A central ingredient of any use of social media is providing an opportunity for feedback. Every church website and church Facebook page should provide space for congregational members and others to share their reactions to what is happening in the parish, make comments on sermons, and raise questions about what the church believes. In contrast to a top-down method of communication, social media thrives on participation and relationship. The image here would be the cocktail party or coffee hour. Facebook does this better than any other form of social media. Your parish wants to aim for transparency about what it is doing and should invite comments and feedback, even if some of that may be negative. People who are interested in your church are not interested in "the party line" and they don't expect your website or Facebook page to simply be a sanitized ad for all the wonderful things your church is doing. They want to connect and interact if they are members, and nonmembers will want to monitor you as a way of verifying that your community can be trusted and that it "practices what it preaches."

It has been my experience that Facebook is most effective for reaching one's parishioners, whereas Twitter has a greater impact on people more removed from the center of things—the general public, as it used to be called. For example, currently I have about 500 "friends" on Facebook. I know who all of them are. Of those 500, about 100 post on a regular basis, and I make a habit of commenting on their posts, even if that is nothing more than a "like" response to something they have shared. Of the approximately 2,000 people who are following me on Twitter, my guess is that I actually know only about 20 percent of them. That means that when I post a tweet, I am broadcasting to an unknown audience. One futurist remarks: "Every time you tweet, one third of your followers are from a country not your own." My comments may have a more subtle impact, but I also need to be much more careful of what I say.

Two other comments about using Facebook and Twitter. The first is the positive effect that a leader's use of these media has on his or her constituency. A comment made to me once by Bishop Andy Doyle of Texas, who is probably more active on social media than any other bishop in the American Church, is to the point. "In the old days, people saw the bishop once a year for about an hour. Now, thanks to social media, those who want can have me in their lives every day. That can make a huge difference in the way they think of the office of bishop, and it gives me a tremendous opportunity to have an impact on their spiritual lives."[13] The English equivalent to Bishop Doyle is the bishop of Buckingham, Allen Wilson, whose daily blogging comments are often picked up by the British press.

Both of these bishops, and others who take time to use social media, have realized another important lesson, highlighted for us by Elizabeth Drescher in her book: Listening on social media is even more important than talking. Her argument might be summarized, "post less, and comment more."[14] Our audience is less interested in whatever brilliant ideas we as bishops, or rectors and vicars may have, than the fact they know that we are taking an interest in their lives and cheering them on from the sidelines. So instead of posting our latest musing on the church—better left for the blogging format anyway—take time to wish your Facebook friends a happy birthday or congratulate them on making the honor role. It doesn't take much time to hit the "like" button.

Another essential element of social media, well described by Elizabeth Drescher and others, is that social media is not just an extension of broadcast media. Those forms of communication, which all of us grew up with, use electronic media like radio and television to deliver a top-down message: a few people addressing hundreds, or thousands, or millions. This approach is the electronic equivalent of a speaker in an auditorium addressing a large audience. But social media works completely differently. It uses a line of communication unlike print media (author to reader, one to one) or broadcast media (speaker to audience, one to many). Instead, the social media flowchart goes one to five to one to fifty to two to a hundred, and so on. This fact makes it highly effective for church communities. Drescher drives home this point when she compares the web presence of a large evangelical megachurch that boasts thousands on its rolls with that of a small midwestern Lutheran congregation with a couple of hundred members. The megachurch site is expensive and glitzy with professionally produced content and pictures that focus primarily on the teachings of the senior pastor rather than on the interaction of members. It is based on the older broadcast model. The little

Lutheran church, however, is much simpler in its presentation. The fact that it is the work of in-house amateurs makes it all the more interesting and attractive. Surprisingly, a far greater percentage of its members make use of the site than the megachurch's members do of their site.[15] Here is an instance where smaller is better.

I haven't said much about an older form of web media, the blog. If you blog yourself, or follow someone who does, you will recognize blogging as belonging to that broadcast genre discussed above. Spending a lot of time blogging is probably a good investment for a church leader if you happen to be an especially insightful thinker, but you will probably get more bang for your buck by posting more frequent short comments and responses on Facebook or Twitter. Again, your followers are much more interested in your relationship and social interaction with them than they are in your penetrating analysis of theology or church politics. Even so, a well-crafted blog can allow a parish priest to reach a far larger audience than would ever be the case on Sunday morning. The former dean of our cathedral, now bishop of Rhode Island, Nicholas Knisely, is a long-time blogger known for his interesting views on science and religion. Depending on his topic, he is likely to have an Internet audience ten to one hundred times larger online than he will on a Sunday morning.

Finally, a caveat. Obviously I am greatly excited about the opportunities the digital age is making available to those of us in the church. Never before in our history have we been able to reach so many with the gospel message so easily and effectively. For a church leader to spend a good chunk of time each day at their computer networking with members and potential members is surely a good investment of time (although one can probably expect to take some heat from congregants who don't understand what may seem an inordinate amount of time spent at one's desk). But as is always the case, there can be too much of a good thing. I have seen cases of clergy who have used Internet technology to inadvertently isolate themselves from their congregations. A post on Facebook has its place, but it can never replace that intimate face-to-face visit in the hospital. A good blog message can put you on the map, but it cannot replace a well-crafted sermon on Sunday morning. A response to a parishioner's tweet can build a bond between you, but so can a phone call in time of need. And whatever you do, don't wear out the electronic welcome mat. A Facebook message or two a day plus several tweets is quite enough. Any more and you may appear to be a pest and may end up getting yourself "unfriended."

The sixth-century revolution in communication embodied in the St. Augustine Gospels ought to do more than simply encourage us to make use of the new media outlets the digital age has gifted us. It also reminds us that such new technologies are also, well, fun. We should not overlook the "wow" factor that must have been present when Augustine or one of his fellow monks pointed to his Gospel book during Mass and said, "Look, here is Jesus!" We can picture the crowd of new converts pressing around, straining to get a better look. The novelty of its presentation made it that much more magical. Like many people, I am always intrigued with the latest gizmo, special effect, or clever Super Bowl ad. Such new approaches make me sit up and take notice, and often bring a smile to my face, no matter the product being sold or the message being pushed.

As every advertising "Mad Man" knows, if you can attract people's attention, they will listen to what you have to say, and attracting their attention means a constant quest after the new, the unique, the sensory, the compelling image. We call this approach "audience appeal." St. Augustine's listeners probably called it magic.

We in the church certainly don't want to conform to Madison Avenue standards, but that does not mean that we need to continue to make our own presentations of the gospel message downright boring. There is a popular website with the apt title of "www.churchmarketingsucks.org," and the name rings true. Often we operate under the myth that just because we are engaged in a spiritual enterprise, we don't have to pay any attention to standards of appearance and presentation that any small business would take for granted. Sadly, our buildings and worship spaces are beset by poor lighting, uncomfortable pews, jerry-rigged public address systems, and grumpy ushers. We pass out bulletins that include nothing of visual interest, set in unreadably small type, and jammed with insider jargon. In all but the largest congregations, we are apt to be asked to sing theologically dubious hymns set to eighteenth-century harmonies by dead white guys, accompanied by a choir of what my old rector used to call "bosom-y sopranos, accompanied by a broken-down piano player." No wonder the folks in the pews don't come back!

Our 1,400-year-old Gospel book may not look like much now, but it offers us a lesson in the importance of being creative and engaging when it comes to worship, of making sure that those who show up on Sunday morning aren't exposed to the "same old, same old," and that we in church leadership offer them something which challenges their minds and their senses, which shakes them up a bit and helps them see the glory of holiness in sometimes surprising ways. Maybe that means a mixed media presentation instead of a sermon, or a question and answer time instead of a lecture, or holding a worship service in the park instead of the church. Yes, church ought to be more than just "fun," but if it is not engaging, attention getting, and transformational, then what is the point? For many of our congregations, fun would be a good place to start. There are so many ways that we can say to our people, "Look, here is Jesus!" that they can only say in return, "Wow!"

The purpose of these past several pages has not been to offer a do-it-yourself guide to social media in the church. There are many excellent treatments of this subject for those interested. These suggestions are meant simply to show what might await us in the church were we to embrace the new opportunities provided by social media. The lesson the St. Augustine Gospels gives the church for today is simply this: When it comes to new ways of making Christ known, go for it! MS 286 introduced a visual approach to an aural culture. Today's digital world supplants the analog universe of broadcast media, which was top-down, didactic, hierarchical, and authoritarian. The digital world is democratic, intuitive, and relational. It is the kind of world that the church needs to learn to feel comfortable in. And it is a world in which the church must constantly reinvent itself as it seeks to witness to the gospel.

The great German theologian Karl Barth was fond of saying, "*Ecclesia semper reformanda*"—the church must always be reformed. Digital guru Don Tapscott puts it this way, "The social world is transforming the way we create wealth, work, learn, play, raise our children, and probably the way we think."[16] The brave new world of social media is here to stay. Will the church be part of it?

— IV —

Continuity

The archbishop was doing what he loved best, inspecting the books in his library at Lambeth Palace. He had decided some months ago to make a bequest of his most valuable books and manuscripts to his beloved Corpus Christi College. Looking back on his long career as priest, college master, and finally as archbishop, he realized with a certain pang that his happiest days had been spent among the book presses in his college's library. He could do no better than share with the scholars there some of his own collection. He called to his assistant John Day to help him go over the final list. "We want to make sure we don't send them any of the archiepiscopal volumes by mistake," he joked.

John had thoughtfully set out on long trestle tables those books and manuscripts he was pretty sure belonged to his master. Both men suspected that the day was not long off when the disposition of the archbishop's possessions would be made public and they wanted no mistakes. John checked the list while the archbishop handled each of the leather-bound books. Some volumes were checked off quickly, others he fingered lovingly, thumbing through their starchy vellum pages, occasionally giving a sigh of pleasure over an especially well-gilded initial letter or a whimsical brightly colored illumination. John could tell which were the archbishop's favorites by how long he paused; it was almost as if he were saying good-bye to old friends.

There was, of course, the huge Bible from Bury with its vivid pictures—it took up almost a whole table by itself. Much less impressive looking but just as dear were those works in the ancient language of King Alfred, the *Chronicle,* a translation of Bede's *Ecclesiastical History of the English People,* and the Saxon King's own translation of Pope Gregory's *Pastoral Care.* The archbishop paused, picked up the *Chronicle,* and read a few sentences out loud, just to see if John was paying attention and to test his fluency in the ancient tongue: *"Her Gregorius papa sende to Brytene Augustinum. mid wel manegum munecum. þe Godes word Engla ðeoda godspelledon."* There were lots of printed books too, including some of the very earliest Bible commentaries and editions of the church fathers. Amazingly to John, the archbishop had actually read most of them. John could easily tell, since so many of them were marked in their margins and underlined with the archbishop's characteristic red crayon.

No wonder he loved them all so much. Each one had a story to tell of how it was obtained. John had heard many times how the archbishop had sent his agents throughout England to beg, borrow, or steal (for what owner was going to say no to the archbishop of Canterbury?) the books he was searching for, particularly those books that would prove to the world that the Church of England was not some new invention, but was the One Holy Catholic and Apostolic Church, rooted in the faith and practice of Jesus's first followers.

When they came to one old Gospel book, the archbishop paused even longer. "I wonder if our predecessor Theodore of blessed memory brought this with him when he came to Canterbury so long ago? It certainly is old. I admit it caught my eye because it was bound with some documents relating to Canterbury, but I've always wondered about it." He passed the volume to John. "Did you ever know John of Essex, the last abbot at St. Augustine's in Canterbury? Good man. I will always be thankful that he thought to send it to me before Thomas Cromwell's agents ransacked the library, although it appears that he was too late to save some of the illuminated pages—sliced out for quick sale, no doubt. Abbot John always had a good eye for books. I am glad he saved this one."

The light in the great hall was fading, and the bell for vespers had just sounded. "Well John, we had better get to the chapel. I think we are done here. I hope my friends in Cambridge enjoy these as much as I did—see to it, will you?

Like many libraries, what would become known as the Parker Library at Corpus Christi College at Cambridge University had a purpose: to prove to Christendom the continuity between the Apostolic Church and the Church of England. Although Archbishop Parker was probably only dimly aware of the importance of the St. Augustine Gospels when he acquired it, we can now think of it as embodying more than any other work in his collection the connection between the ancient church, centered on Rome and replanted on English soil by Augustine, and the newly formed "*Ecclesia Anglicana*," now governed by Augustine's successor, Matthew Parker himself. His library was to be the intellectual glue that held the two historical embodiments of Christianity together. It was to prove not only the legitimacy of the Church of England, headed now not by a pope but by a queen, as well as Parker's own primacy as a product of the apostolic succession. In a collection housed in the quiet courtyard of a Cambridge college, both Parker's political career as the first reformed archbishop of the Elizabethan settlement and his intellectual career as scholar of the ancient church were to come together.

Parker's own career was anything but ambitious. He was born in Norwich in 1504, the eldest son of middle-class tradespeople. His mother may have been related through marriage to his later colleague, Archbishop Thomas Cranmer. He belonged to St. Saviour's parish and his baptism is recorded there. He received his earliest grounding in Latin letters locally, and showed enough promise to be sent to Corpus Christi College in 1522. There he distinguished himself academically. He received his Bachelor of Arts degree in 1525 and was quickly elected a fellow two years later, the same year he was ordained to the priesthood. Even before he had finished working on his master's degree, he had come to the attention of Cardinal Thomas Wolsey, who wished to recruit him for the teaching faculty of his newly founded Cardinal College (later Christ Church) at Oxford.

Parker refused this honor. Perhaps because of his growing interest in the work of the German reformers and his evolving Protestant sympathies, he preferred to stay in Cambridge, which was to become a center for religious debate, much of which took place at the White Hart Tavern. The building itself is long gone, but its site, in the shadow of King's College, might well be thought of as the launching pad of the English Reformation.

Although there is evidence that Parker spent more time listening than talking—he managed to stay out of trouble with suspicious university authorities—his reputation as a scholar brought him to the attention of Queen Anne Boleyn, herself noted for her sympathy with Continental reformers. Queen Anne asked to have Parker as her personal chaplain, and the emotional bond was so close that she placed her daughter, the future Queen Elizabeth, in his care just before her execution in May 1536. Years later, Parker declared that "if I had not been so much bound to the mother I would not so soon have granted to serve the daughter." Yet this close connection ultimately led to Parker's elevation to archbishop many years later.

Being chaplain to Queen Anne was not a full-time job, and when Parker was not at court, he served well as the dean of a college of secular canons at St. John's College, Stoke by Clare (the building is still there, now a private school for boys). His work there must have given him plenty of time to further his studies.

It is an indication of Parker's cautious nature that, even after his patroness was executed, he managed to stay in the good graces of King Henry VIII, whom he also served as chaplain. During one of Thomas Cromwell's more ferocious purges, Parker nearly fell from royal favor but was saved by the intercession of Richard Yngworth, bishop of Dover, who advocated before the king that Parker "hath ever been of a good judgment and set forth the Word of God after a good manner. For this he suffers some grudge."[1]

He was soon back in Henry's good graces, who appointed him first as a prebendary (or canon) of Ely Cathedral in 1541, and shortly afterward recommended him to be the new master of his alma mater, Corpus Christi College. His time there, from 1544 to 1553, was to be the happiest time of his life, in spite of the fact that he had a serious run-in with the chancellor of the university, Bishop Stephen Gardiner, over a satirical play put on by some students that ridiculed the more catholic and conservative churchmen of their day, Gardiner himself included.

Thomas Cromwell's efforts to dissolve the monasteries and channel their resources into the royal treasury also extended for a time to university colleges. Fortunately, Parker was appointed to report on the state of the Cambridge establishments, and it was largely due to his intercessions and influence with the king that most of those colleges did not suffer the same fate as monastic houses.

Parker's leadership role in both government and Protestant circles continued to grow. He gained additional preferments, such as the deanship of Lincoln, and became a good friend of Martin Luther's German disciple Martin Bucer. When Bucer died while in exile in England in 1551, Parker preached at his funeral.

When Queen Mary eventually succeeded to the throne in 1553, bringing with her an agenda to restore England to the Roman Catholic fold, Parker, as a leading Protestant thinker, had to abandon his offices and live in domestic exile. With his wife, Margaret Harlestone, whom he had married in 1547 before it was technically legal for clergy to do so, he essentially went "underground," living a very simple life, making every effort to avoid public attention.

With the ascension of Elizabeth I, and the end to the prosecution of the reforming cause, Parker reluctantly moved back into a leadership position. It is no surprise that the new queen should have selected him as her archbishop, although Parker at first strongly resisted.

His actual consecration to that office has long been the subject of controversy. Later Roman Catholic apologists, who have sought to discredit the Church of England, created a myth known as the "Nag's Head Tavern" incident, in which they claimed that Parker had been consecrated at a local disreputable watering hole with no regard for the canonical form for ordination of a bishop, simply by having a Bible pressed on his neck, thus breaking apostolic succession. In fact, there is a very detailed account of Parker's consecration service, which took place at St. Mary's Church in Lambeth on December 19, 1559, with a large number of English bishops participating and the proper liturgical forms scrupulously adhered to. Still, such charges must have abounded even in Parker's day and no doubt made the question of his "legitimacy"—and that of the church he headed—of special concern to him.

It is easy to imagine some of the issues the new archbishop must have faced during his tenure. Under the conciliatory influence of the queen, the new Church of England was fully coming into being, combining elements of traditional catholic liturgical practice with the evangelical concern for Scripture inspired by the Lutheran and Calvinist reformers. Yet the hierarchy of the church itself was in chaos, with bishops and clergy experiencing the whiplash of changing loyalties to Tudor monarchs, each with their own religious agenda.

As archbishop, Parker was a diligent but uninspired administrator. It has been pointed out that he left no great theological tract, collection of sermons, or Prayer Book revision, and that of all fifty-five volumes of material from his episcopacy published by the Parker Society in the nineteenth century, only one is made of up of his (not very interesting) correspondence. Still, he had the confidence of his queen, partly due to his dogged patience and loyalty to her, and she in turn respected and admired him, even though she did not approve of the fact that he was married.

Elizabeth once snubbed Parker's wife at court, claiming that she did not know what to call her: "Madam I may not call you, mistress I am ashamed to call you."[2] Parker himself seems to have been devoted to Margaret. Under the name "Thomas Martin," Parker published a defense of married clergy. His friend and colleague Bishop Edwin Sandys (then of Worcester, later of York) nicknamed Margaret "Parker's Abbess" because of her gravity, chastity, discretion, and piety.

During his tenure, Parker's principal headache was dealing with what has come to be known as the "vestiarian" or "edification" controversy in which the liturgical attire or vestments worn by the clergy became the flash point for a wide range of disagreements over the governance of the church. Anglicans have always been intrigued with vestments—there is probably no more favorite topic among clergy to this day—but in Parker's time the very act of wearing or not wearing a white surplice could be a controversial act. More radical reformers considered such items as copes (worn mostly by bishops) and white surplices (worn by parish clergy) to be examples of superstition and "popery" and refused to use them. To their thinking, since they were not mentioned in the Bible, they had no place in the church.

The edification controversy had its roots in the early days of the English Reformation and takes its name from the passage in 1 Corinthians 14:26 in which Paul (in the English of the Bible Parker would have used) asks, "How is it then brethren? Whan ye come together, euery one hath a psalme, hath doctryne, hath a tunge, hath a reuelacion, hath an interpretacion. Let all be done to edifyenge."[3] This led to speculation about what constituted "essential" aspects of Christian belief and practice and which were "optional" additions for the edification of the faithful; in the technical language of the Reformers, what was essential and what was *adiaphora* (things "indifferent"). Most, but not all, considered such things as church vestments to belong to this latter category. But if there was to be a standard as to what a priest should wear, who had the authority to make that decision?

Queen Elizabeth surely thought she did. In the Act of Uniformity of 1559, it was made clear that the monarch had the authority "to ordeyne and publishe suche further Ceremonies or rites as maye bee most meet for the advancement of Goddes Glorye, the edifieing of his church and the due Reverance of Christes holye mistries and Sacramentes."[4]

The problem was that Elizabeth left it to her archbishop to work out the details. She expected him to enforce her standard (wearing cassock and surplice during divine service, while at Communion, chasuble and copes were also permitted) but never truly backed him up when he tried to enforce this ruling. This made it easy for more Protestant-minded clergy, who liked bishops not at all and vestments even less, to make Parker the target for their frustration with the general state of the church.

Parker did his best. The matter came to a head at a meeting of London clergy at Lambeth on March 26, 1566. At that gathering, Parker arranged for one member of the clergy to appear before the rest dressed in a way he deemed appropriate; there was to be no debate about the decision. The standard was to be a square cap, gown, tippet, and sur-plice. The assembled clergy were instructed that henceforth they were to "inviolably observe the rubric of the Book of Common Prayer, and the Queen Majesty's injunctions: and the Book of Convocation."[5] The clergy were ordered to commit themselves on the spot, in writing, by signing a statement with the words *volo* or *nolo*. Sixty-one agreed, but thirty-seven refused and were immediately suspended and deprived of their livings.

It seems an extreme step for what may appear to us a minor matter of personal taste. But Parker correctly sur-mised that what was really at stake was the governance of the church. Would it be ruled by the monarch and bishops or by a Presbyterian or Congregationalist polity, as the non-conformists desired? He was convinced that if the dissenters were to have their way, the very foundations of English soci-ety would collapse and that the agenda of those who would become the English Puritans would eventually bring down the Queen herself.

Parker, however, really had no stomach for these battles, which were hardly settled in his own lifetime. He avoided political confrontation whenever he could, and declined to attend the meetings of the Privy Council. He died in 1575 without resolving any of the issues he had inherited. His rather clumsy attempts to address the underlying problems through heavy-handed pronouncements but without the active support of the queen only led to further animosities between "catholics" and "puritans" that took decades to resolve. Indeed there are those who claim that the Church of England has never resolved them, as evidenced by the continued struggle in the Anglican Communion over the interpretation of Scripture, the inclusion of women and gay and lesbian members in the governance of the church, and the exclusivity of Jesus as the path to salvation.

As a church leader, Parker proved himself hard working and conscientious, but he was cautious and ineffectual when it came to dealing with the pressing issues of his day. He was, after all, an ecclesiological survivor who had lived through multiple changes of monarchs and church polities. He had managed to flourish while some of his more courageous and outspoken colleagues had suffered martyrdom for their faith.

Parker might have been timid and vacillating as a politician, but his scholarly insights were clear and far-reaching. Parker was possessed by an understanding of the history of the church that would prove foundational to the rise of Anglicanism. For him the time period between the arrival of St. Augustine until the Norman conquest (597–1066) was the high-water mark of the English Church. The Anglo-Saxon church for Parker was the English Church *par excellence*—hence his interest in all things Anglo-Saxon. In his view, the English Church was in full conformity with the church of the apostles. The enemy in his mind was the papacy (Pope Gregory was an exception since he was the impulse behind St. Augustine's mission). For the most part, the pope at Rome had done nothing but subvert and exploit the English Church. To use a modern analogy, Rome had slowly forced an independent and spiritually vital church to join a European religious common market, run by the pope. The English Church, with its ruggedly independent Anglo-Saxon leadership (exemplified for Parker by the great monk-bishops like Chad, Dunstan, and Wulfstan), had become increasingly fed up with this foreign interference, finally rejecting it altogether under Henry VIII.

But even more central to Parker's understanding of the church was his assertion that this break did not mean a rejection of what we would call the "core values" of the church. The English Reformation was simply a return to the teaching of the apostles, and the reestablishment of ancient faith of the primitive church. The Church of England, the *Ecclesia Anglicana*, was nothing new. Rather it was the current and purest expression of the Christian faith.

Parker made his points not in works of theology, but in the form of a work of history, whose very title proclaims Parker's thesis—*De Antiquitate Ecclesiae (On the Antiquity of the Church)*. The work, first published in 1572, set out to prove the continuity of Parker's church with that of those who landed on the shores of Kent in 597. *De Antiquitate* proved to be a quite popular, although rather unoriginal, work. It consists largely of short biographies of each of the archbishops of Canterbury, beginning with Augustine and leading to his own time. His introductory comments are the most interesting part of the book. Here he sets out his views on the continuity of the church with its ancient roots. He claims that the English were evangelized, not by the efforts of the pope but by Joseph of Arimathea, whose legendary visit to Glastonbury Parker firmly believed. "Joseph did not receive his faith from the Pope, but from the Lord." Parker believes his reason for writing is to establish that ancient connection to Jesus's followers ("*A quibus Evangelica luce primum illustratam Britanniam supra commemoravimus*"). St. Augustine and his immediate successors are the heroes, and monarchical popes like Innocent III are the villains. Even Pope Gregory, who initiated the English mission, takes a backseat to Augustine, whose "humanity" conquered the "institutional Christianity of Gregory ("*Ita Christianitem et institutum Gregorii, vicit humanitas Augustini*").[6]

Although Parker's views are fanciful, to say the least, his apologetic for an indigenous, "national" church, independent of Roman control, helped create what one scholar has called a "myth of Anglicanism," which affects our understanding of the church to this day.

Parker paid for at least part of his work himself, commissioning in 1566 the printer John Day to cut in brass the first Anglo-Saxon typeface for a publication showing "the ancient faith of the Church of England touching the Sacrament of the Body and Blood of the Lord . . . above 600 years ago." In addition to its historical introduction, Parker argued that it was medieval innovations that forbade the clergy to marry and that restricted receiving at Communion to one kind. In a sense, *De Antiquitate* was not just a work of theology or history. It was the summation of Parker's life work. He was, as his earliest biographer states, "a mighty collector of books,"[7] not as a mere bibliophile but for a practical purpose, to help the Church of England in its struggle against Rome and the Puritans, and to provide intellectual ammunition for the policies of the monarch he served. It is no wonder a surviving presentation copy of the book made especially for Queen Elizabeth shows signs of being well used.

As Parker's role as a church administrator became more frustrating and difficult, he turned his attention to his library. At one point he had urged the queen to assemble a great national library, but getting no response, Parker set to work to create his own. He obtained from the Privy Council an order that allowed him to examine and "borrow" all books and manuscripts collected from recently dissolved monasteries. One of his agents in this task, Stephan Bateman, collected 6,700 such items during a four-year period.

The archbishop's palace at Lambeth was turned into a veritable research institution, employing a sizable staff. "I have within my house in wages, drawers, cutters, painters, limners, writers, and bookbinders. . . . I toy out my time partly with copying of books, partly in devising ordinance for scholars, to help the ministry, partly in genealogies, and so forth."[8]

His library assistants were capable men. John Day, already mentioned, was a London printer of note. And they were well paid. "I gave to Sir Thomas Josselin's brother, an antiquary in my house, a prebend worth 30 pounds and procured for him 300 pounds," a substantial amount.[9]

There was little in the way of book production in his day that did not come to Parker's attention. The records of the London Stationer's Company lists Parker as one who licensed books for publication. This is no surprise, since censorship was expected of any potentially dangerous religious works, and who better to exercise it than the archbishop himself?

Parker simply delegated scholarly work to his subordinates. He took an active role as well, editing such works as Aelfric's *Homilies of the Anglo-Saxon Church* and Matthew Paris's *Chronica Major.* Anglo-Saxon works especially interested Parker, coming from the time period when in his view the church was least corrupted by Roman influences.

No doubt it was during this time that Parker first considered leaving his work to the place he was happiest, Corpus

Christi College in Cambridge. He realized the importance of his collection and wanted to make sure it would survive into the future in one piece. Under the provisions of his will, he left about 400 manuscripts and 1,000 more printed works to his college, with strict provision that they were to be kept together. The conditions for Parker's bequest, honored to this day, was that there must be a regular accounting of all materials. (With no modern borrowing systems, and with books being extremely valuable, theft from medieval libraries was a common occurrence.) If any books were found to be missing, the entire library was to be forfeited, first to Gonville and Caius College, and if they were not up to the task, then to Trinity Hall. Incidentally, the same terms applied to a gift of silver plate Parker left to the college. The result is that both books and silver have remained intact, although the current head of the Parker Library, Dr. de Hamel, confesses to a certain anxiety each time the holdings are inventoried! "Every year my assistant and I hold our breaths, and make a careful count. So far so good!"

It was perhaps because of these exacting terms that over the years the Parker Library has gained a reputation among scholars for being nearly inaccessible. Up until the early years of the twentieth century, it required three separate keys held by three different fellows of the College to unlock the collection. Dr. de Hamel recalls that as a graduate student, he himself was refused access to one of the library's manuscripts. No wonder that under his custodianship, the Parker collection has become far more accessible, with all of its holdings now available online in digitalized form through a joint project with Stanford University (https://parkerweb.stanford.edu).

We have been focusing on Parker's role as an antiquarian with the distinct mission of cementing the connection between the "primitive church" and the newly formed Church of England. But his accomplishments were even more far reaching and deserve mention.

Parker deserves a place of honor in the process of creating an English Bible, which would culminate with the publication of the Authorized or King James Version in 1611. Parker's contribution came in the form of the so-called "Bishops' Bible," which he proposed, prepared, and published in 1572. Even though this Bible was to be famous (or infamous) for its inaccuracies, it was an important part of the genealogy of that later Bible, which was to have such a monumental impact on English theology, language, and even politics.

Parker also gave considerable attention to the 1559 revision of the Book of Common Prayer, especially to the language of the psalter. In the Parker Library there is a copy of corrections to the Thirty-Nine Articles, along with the queen's suggestions for the same. These corrections helped formed the basis of the version approved by the clergy in 1562.

We in the church thus owe a debt of gratitude to Matthew Parker, a figure whose contributions are often overshadowed by his predecessor and friend, Thomas Cranmer. Even though as a church leader he was often timid and as a thinker lacked in originality and depth, he was a loyal and hard-working preserver of our historical heritage as Anglicans, and had a decisive role in helping to create for our church a lasting identity. Key for him and for us today was the concept of continuity, the unbroken connection we have with all catholic Christians, the tradition we share with all the faithful for all eternity.

Every Sunday evening for the past fifty years, a large group of young people has gathered at St. Mark's Episcopal Cathedral in Seattle. Here in the dim candlelit vastness of this great gothic-style building, they listen for an hour to the soaring sounds not of rock music but of ancient Gregorian chant. Many bring their own pillows and lie on the floor listening. There are no words in the service, no prayers, Scripture readings, or sermons, just thousand-year-old songs of worship. Almost none of the young people there would call themselves Episcopalians, nor do many see themselves as Christians in any traditional sense. What brings them week after week at 9:30 at night is a sense of the transcendent, and a connection with an ancient form of worship.[10]

The St. Mark's service is just one example of the growing interest in the liturgical practices of the early church. In many parish churches today, one can find other such expressions of the ancient church's worship, such as icons, walking the labyrinth, centering prayer, the Daily Office, use of chant, votive candles, *lectio divina,* and people living together in monastic-style communities.

This rediscovery of ancient liturgical practice is the most public expression of rekindled interest in continuity with the early church. This interest often comes under the heading of the "emerging church," a movement that is interested in far more than just corporate worship. Yet just like the Oxford Movement of the nineteenth century, whose doctrine of the church was given public expression in such "high church" practices as frequent communion, candles on the altar, and the wearing of priestly vestments, so the ecclesiology of the emerging church movement is evidenced in worship styles that are rooted in the church's earliest history.

Historian Diana Butler Bass suggests in her provocative study *The Practicing Congregation* that this desire to reconnect with ancient tradition, to create "a new old church," is a healthy path forward for many churches. She calls congregations that have embraced this pattern "practicing congregations." Such congregations are "retraditioning" around liturgical worship, lifelong Christian formation, and intentional engagement with the needs of the community.

> Retraditioning is a simpler concept than its awkward name implies. It is a process wherein individuals—and congregations—are responding to the larger cultural results of modern fragmentation by creating

communities that provide sacred space for the formation of identity and meaning, the construction of "pock-
ets" of connectedness to the longer history of Christian
witness and practice in a disconnected world.[11]

Bass's work was published about the same time as
forward-thinking parishes in a host of different denominations were putting such ideas into practice in a movement
that came to be called the "emerging church." She had correctly described "the edge of a trend whereby religious communities focus on meaning making by gathering up the past
and re-presenting it through both story and action in ways
that help people connect with God."[12]

This trend or movement is notoriously hard to define,
but a good place to start would be with Eddie Gibbs and
Ryan Bolger's description in their book, *Emerging Churches:
Creating Christian Community in Postmodern Cultures*:
"Emerging churches are communities that practice the
way of Jesus within postmodern cultures. Their definition
encompasses nine practices: Emerging churches (1) identify with the life of Jesus, (2) transform the secular realm,
and (3) live highly communal lives. Because of these three
activities, they (4) welcome the stranger, (5) serve with gen-
erosity, (6) participate as producers, (7) create as created
beings, (8) lead as a body, and (9) take part in spiritual activities."[13] No mention of novel worship practices here! A less
formal definition comes from early advocate Tony Jones,
who states simply, "The Emerging Church was founded to

get the evangelical church to take art, social justice and other what might be considered progressive issues more seriously. It was also founded to get the Mainline church to loosen their neckties a little bit."[14]

Historically, the emerging church movement might be thought of as part of an ongoing reformation process famously described by Phyllis Tickle in *The Great Emergence: How Christianity Is Changing and Why*. Her thesis, further developed in subsequent writings, was that major shifts in church belief and practice happen approximately every five hundred years: the era of church consolidation under Gregory the Great in the sixth century, the Great Schism of the eleventh century, and the Reformation of the sixteenth century. According to Tickle, "Every five hundred years, the church cleans out its attic and has a giant rummage sale." We are now, she believes, in the midst of such a seismic change as the dogmas and structures of organized Christianity, our inheritance from the medieval and Reformation churches, are giving way to "fresh expressions" of the faith.[15]

Ever since the adjectives "emergent" and "emerging" were first applied to the church around 1989, they have been appropriated by a wide variety of theologians and traditions. Although the words "emerging" and "emergent" are often used interchangeably, the latter is associated with a formal organization, Emergent Village, while the former is used to describe an ongoing "conversation" among progressive church leaders of varying stripes. According to the

Wikipedia definition, there are at least three main streams of emergent church thought:

- *Relevants* are theological conservatives who are interested in updating to current culture. They look to people like Dan Kimball and Donald Miller.
- *Reconstructionists* are generally theologically evangelical, and speak of new forms of church that result in transformed lives. [Included in this group are also those who are interested in the house church movement.] They look to Neil Cole, Michael Frost, and Alan Hirsch.
- *Revisionists* are theologically liberal and openly question whether evangelical doctrine is appropriate for the postmodern world. They look to leaders such as Brian McLaren, Rob Bell, and Doug Pagitt.[16]

The emerging church movement has its roots in "postmodern" thinking, another very difficult term to describe exactly. According to D. A. Carson in *Becoming Conversant with the Emerging Church*:

Modernism is often pictured as pursuing truth, absolutism, linear thinking, rationalism, certainty, the cerebral as opposed to the effective—which in turn breeds arrogance, and inflexibility, the lust to be right, the desire to control. Postmodernism, by contrast, recognizes how much of what we "know" is shaped by the culture in which we live, is controlled by emotions and aesthetics and heritage, and in fact can only be intelligently held as part of a common tradition, without overbearing claims to be true or right.[17]

Emerging church therefore appears whenever traditional evangelistic efforts are made to accommodate such postmodern thinking. Hence anything that would seem to teach "absolute truth" (including a literalist approach to the Bible) or tends to be overly dogmatic, sectarian, or rigid is rejected in favor of open inquiry; community building; looser, less systematic teaching; and a worship style that makes use of visual methods, storytelling, and more expressive word and music instead of absolute truths delivered from the pulpit and Bible study.

What all these various emergent churches have in common is a desire to apply the traditions, teachings, and practices of the "inherited church" to postmodern culture. By modeling their "emergent" church on what they perceived as the foundation of the ancient, apostolic, or "primitive" church, they echo Archbishop Parker's concern with reestablishing the connection between the church of their own day with the church of the apostles.

At first this quest among new and often young Christians for continuity with the ancient church might seem counterintuitive. Those of us who have been involved in our churches for a long time naturally assume that young people are looking for "contemporary" expressions of the faith, where praise band music and digital media are front and center. It seems this is only partly true, and that it may be an assumption that reflects our own "boomer" tastes rather than those of twenty- and thirty-year-olds. When it comes to worship style, my own (boomer) generation tends to like show—bright lights, big crowds, high production values. The megachurch ethos naturally appeals to this audience. That audience, however, is now in decline as younger folks begin to look to smaller and more intimate ways to gather, to worship, and, especially, to live out their Christian beliefs in everyday life. They don't trust big crowds and charismatic leaders, while too much liturgical choreography strikes them as pretentious and "phony."

Sociologists point out that these shifts reflect the tastes of younger generations, usually referred to as "Gen X" (born from about 1960 to 1980) and "Millennials" or "Gen Y" (born from about 1980 to 2000), who tend to be more socially liberal and distrustful of institutions and who value relationships within small groups more than their parents. In religious matters especially, they admit to being less likely to believe in God, or to have any need for organized religion, than any previous group in history.

Emergent churches are more likely to appeal to these age groups than "mainline" denominations. Yet notably, many such new churches also consciously include practices from traditional churches that at first glance might seem outmoded or "old school." Dan Kimball, a young Baptist preacher and writer about church renewal, counsels church planters in his book *The Emerging Church: Vintage Christianity for New Generations* to make sure that the decor of their new worship space is appropriately "churchy." No one wants to look at folding chairs and fluorescent lights when they can have stained glass and candles! The best building you can find for a new church, he advises, is an old one, a place that even new Christians can recognize as being a holy place.[18]

To share a personal example, a few years ago I attended a service at the Imago Dei Community, an "emergent-style" evangelical church in Portland, Oregon (http://idcpdx. com). Until recently this group met in a high school auditorium. Its congregation is made up of mostly young singles and couples. The attitude is informal; the pastor, Rick McKinley, sits in the congregation until it is time for him to speak, which he does wearing a polo shirt, shorts, and sandals (it was summer in Portland). I found it interesting that even the word "church" is suspect for this congregation, even though they long for a "community" of faith. But although the attitude was casual and "untraditional," the music and liturgy were not. The auditorium has been carefully decorated with fabric and, with the lights turned low, the front of the church glowed with hundreds of candles surrounding chalices of wine and plates of unleavened bread to be used later for communion. The music was simple and moving: meditative Celtic-style melodies played on a flute with acoustic guitar accompaniment. No hard rock here! Instead the entire service was done almost in a Taizé fashion with plenty of time for quiet reflection. This approach incorporates the "vintage faith" that authors like Dan Kimball are advocating. I admit I found this approach refreshing.

What are these young people looking for? For a sense of the divine surely, but one that they find by a connection to an ancient tradition, represented in modern guise. I think that Archbishop Parker would have approved. He would have liked the slogan one often finds in such congregations—"The way to the future is through the past."

Although this slogan is well known to younger evangelicals, its message still has not penetrated very far into Episcopal churches. This is ironic, for our denomination embodies just the ancient approach these evangelicals seem to long for. We would do well to pay attention to the ancient/future church movement, which began nearly forty years ago, well in advance of emergent congregations, and has influenced a whole generation of evangelical church leaders.

The architect of this movement was a former fundamentalist pastor and theologian who spent most of his career drifting toward Anglicanism. His name was Robert E. Webber and his teaching, plus the more than forty books he published, led to the founding of several think tanks, including the Robert E. Weber Institute for Worship Studies (www.iwsfla.org). He stirred up a hornet's nest of controversy in the American evangelical movement that has shown no sign of dying down.

Webber (1933–2007) was born to Baptist missionary parents and graduated from the conservative Bob Jones University, but he eventually earned degrees at Anglican, Presbyterian, and Lutheran seminaries. He is most associated with the two institutions where he taught: Wheaton College and the Northern Baptist Theological Seminary.

His autobiography, *Evangelicals on the Canterbury Trail: Why Evangelicals Are Attracted to the Liturgical Church*, recounts his personal journey from fundamentalism to his decision to join the Episcopal Church.[19] Once an Episcopalian, he in turn called that church back to its evangelical roots, and for that reason he has received much attention from the so-called Anglican groups that split with the Episcopal Church after 2003 during the Bishop Gene Robinson controversy. (Webber, however, never left the Episcopal Church.)

All of Webber's work centers on some common themes:

1. Historically, the church did not begin with the Reformation. Christians need to be rooted in the legacy of the medieval church and especially of the early church fathers as well as its Jewish liturgical roots.

2. Modern worship should include all historical expressions, from ancient chant to Pentecostal fervor. He called this "blended worship." However, that worship must always affirm the Trinity, the divinity of Jesus, and the Bible. "There is only one kind of worship, Biblical worship."[20] This blending of worship traditions is often called "convergence," and it is succinctly defined by one of Webber's followers: Ancient future worship is the convergence, in one act of worship, of historic and contemporary streams of worship. It usually builds on

the default worship stream of the particular worshiping community.[21] In practical terms that might mean that a nonliturgical church might start doing such things as celebrating the Eucharist more often, or observing the Lenten season. For a traditional church it might mean a greater use of liturgical art or icons, building a labyrinth, or using incense on a regular basis.

3. The church needs to reject enlightenment rationalism and reemphasize transcendence and mystery. He wrote: "The story of Christianity moves from a focus on mystery in the classic period, to institution in the medieval era, to individualism in the Reformation era, to reason in the modern era, and now, in the postmodern era, back to mystery."[22]

4. Christianity must disassociate itself from modernism and become a countercultural and prophetic presence in society. It can never accommodate itself to paganism but must be "an alternative practice of life." "Christians in a postmodern world will succeed, not by watering down the faith, but by being a countercultural community that invites people to be shaped by the story of Israel and of Jesus."[23]

5. We must move beyond differences in Christian creeds, practices, and structure to find our common roots as Christians. He called for us to move beyond labels like "liberal" and "conservative," to practice what Brian McClaren would call "a generous orthodoxy." "We must learn from each other, affirming that we all stand in the

historic faith as we seek to understand it and apply it to the new world in which we minister."[24]

I rarely visit a church in my diocese that has not in the past decade or so begun practices associated with emerging churches. To an older generation these might have been viewed as "high church" excesses, but they now appear in congregations across the liturgical spectrum. For example, in the Diocese of Arizona:

- A parish in a retirement community built an outdoor labyrinth, heavily used by nonmembers.
- Icons now flank the high altar of two new church buildings.
- A retired classics professor offers a popular weekday night class in New Testament Greek.
- At least ten parishes offer a regular Taizé worship. Several others are experimenting with Celtic services.
- A new church plant of inner-city youth features both rap music and incense at its services.
- The topic of the annual deacon's retreat is centering prayer.

From conversations with my fellow bishops, I know that this search for continuity with the ancient church is common throughout this country. For liturgical churches, this quest began with the liturgical renewal movement of the 1950s. Beginning with Roman Catholic scholars on the Continent and spreading to Anglican Churches in England and

America, this movement sought to emphasize the Eucharist as "the principal act of Christian worship." The work of Dom Gregory Dix, for example, had a huge impact on the revision of the Book of Common Prayer in the Episcopal Church in the 1970s. Liturgical scholars also researched and advocated that this sacrament be performed as it was done in the earliest days of the church. In just sixty years, our liturgical style has changed from clergy wearing surplice and stole and officiating at Morning Prayer on most Sundays to priests wearing medieval-style vestments and offering the sacrament several times a week.

So what are the lessons that we in the modern church can learn from Parker's use of the St. Augustine Gospels to establish continuity with the ancient church in his own day?

The adjective "nimble" has been bantered about much in recent years in studies of church structures. The Episcopal Church, for example, recently engaged in a deliberate self-study process under the direction of a Task Force on Reimagining the Episcopal Church. The final report of that study was presented to the General Convention of 2015. In the discussions leading up to that report one finds a strong sense that the church needs to be more flexible—more nimble—in responding to cultural and social change.

The Episcopal Church's structures and governance processes reflect assumptions from previous eras that do not always fit with today's contexts. They have not adapted to the rapidly changing cultural, political, and social environments in which we live. The churchwide structures and governance processes are too disconnected from local needs and too often play a "gating" or regulatory role to local innovation. They are often too slow and confusing to deal decisively with tough and urgent tradeoffs or to pursue bold directions that must be set at the churchwide level.[25]

The changes we face are not nearly as daunting as those Archbishop Parker did at the time of the English Reformation. However, the rate of change of our culture is just as fast, and just as far-reaching. Old structures of church governance often lack the agility to respond quickly enough to the needs of a "wired" society. General Convention itself is a lumbering and expensive legislative dinosaur, created in the day when delegates traveled by train and communication was done by printing press and letter. Two local church institutions are just as outmoded. One is the diocesan convention, whose modes of meeting and voting also reflect nineteenth-century assumptions. The interaction of delegates is governed by *Robert's Rules of Order,* written in 1876! The assumption is that decision-making must be the product of conflict and debate rather than consensus. There must be a better way to make policy and build diocesan-wide relationships. Another outmoded structure is the process leading up to ordination, overseen by a Commission on Ministry, which normally takes years and costs thousands of dollars. What remains to be seen is whether or not the machinery of church governance can reform itself from within, becoming open to these changes that will require the scrapping of old, beloved patterns of behavior.

We also learn from Archbishop Parker that the process of change requires close attention to cultural norms. It was part of his task to build a national church that responded to the assumptions of early modern English culture. These were utterly different than those of the late-medieval Roman Catholic Church, which had no room for such concepts as nationalism, vernacular printed communication, the rise of the middle class, and the colonization of new peoples and territories. In our time the church faces the even more daunting issues of a global economy, instant digital communication, and shrinking resources. We live in a world that is both complex but highly interconnected. Ironically, in Parker's age people were rediscovering that the world was round. In our time, to use Thomas Friedman's famous phrase, we have rediscovered that the world is flat!

Within this societal flux, there is still the need for faithfulness to the gospel. This is precisely what Parker believed himself to be doing, recasting the teaching and practice of the church in ways that were faithful to the church of the apostles, purifying it from the accretions and corruptions of the medieval church. His targets were papal supremacy, the cult of saints, priestly prerogative, and liturgical excess. Those involved with the emerging church movement have their own list of teaching and practices they would like to junk, including such doctrines as original sin and penal substitutionary atonement (the idea that Jesus had to die on the cross to save us), church hierarchies, outmoded creeds, and music written by dead white guys. We too are in the midst of our own reformation. One is reminded of the classic aphorism, *ecclesia semper reformanda*—the church is always to be reformed. The "house cleaning" of the church will always be taking place. What is vital, however, is that in that process the church remain faithful to its core values and to the centrality of the gospel of Jesus Christ. Matthew Parker did his best to reform the church of his day, and so must we.

Matthew Parker was also on a quest for continuity, to show that there was no disconnect between the church of the apostles and the church of his own day, between the *ecclesia anglicana* and the *ecclesia primitiva*. Of course, some of his motivations were political and juridical. There is a marked note of self-justification in his efforts to prove his pedigree on the list of archbishops of Canterbury going back to St. Augustine. But more than simply creating a new status quo, Parker also longs for the stability, the connection, the authority of the ancient church. To be part of that church is to be connected to the apostles and to Jesus himself.

There is a hunger today for this kind of connectedness with the ancient church. Speaking personally, it was this quest for connection with the past that brought me into the Anglican tradition in the first place. When I was an undergraduate in the 1970s there was much interest in discovering one's "roots." This interest was no doubt sparked by Alex

Haley's 1976 bestseller with that title. Although I had been raised in a church family (my dad was a Presbyterian minister), during my first two years of college I went through my agnostic phase, when, after having taken a couple of introductory philosophy courses, I was convinced that Christianity was not worthy of serious intellectual attention. That is until a friend invited me to come with her to a little very high "Anglo Catholic" parish. It was a gem of building, built of dark brick in the Romanesque style, full of icons and sanctuary lamps, and redolent with incense. I liked it so much I went back. I was fascinated by a liturgy and tradition that I had found very little of in the Presbyterian Church, and I was challenged by sermons that focused on the Scriptures and the great theologians of the church.

Although my guess is that young people are not breaking down our doors to become "high church" Episcopalians, there is an attraction here that we would do well to pay attention to. As we have seen above, we have a great inheritance from the ancient church that is in fact very popular, even if it finds its way into church life in a piecemeal fashion. I have been to churches in many different denominations that have a labyrinth in their parking lot, incense on special days, icons carried in procession, and Taizé chants in Latin as part of their Sunday morning worship. As part of the "oldest family on earth," Christians want to know about their spiritual genealogy and the rich practices that they share with their ancestors. Any church that wishes to grow will need to make sure that hunger is being met.

Continuity with the past can be a powerful draw. In the Diocese of Arizona, we have a new experimental mission congregation: St. Jude's. The young men and women in this congregation picked their patron on purpose. Many of them considered themselves "lost causes" before they became Christians. Many have experienced drug addiction, incarceration, teen pregnancy. The vicar of St. Jude's has even performed a baptism by immersion in a swimming pool where the candidate had to keep his foot out of the water since he was wearing an electronic tracking bracelet because he was on probation! Most of the young people in the congregation are recent converts, and few have any experience with the Episcopal Church. Hence, on the eve of my visitation the vicar was explaining to them the role of the bishop, particularly how the bishop was the embodiment of "apostolic succession." "Do you mean," said one seventeen-year-old, "that the hands that ordained Bishop Smith go back all that time to the Apostle's hands? . . . That means that when Bishop Smith puts his hands on my head—it's like Jesus was putting his hands on my head. Cool!"

Sometimes the outward reflections of the quest for continuity with the early church are easier to describe than the quest itself. Another personal anecdote might help.

My second cousin is a young evangelical Christian who lives in Portland, Oregon. He was recently hired as a worship leader for a new nondenominational church plant in that city. Whenever I see him, I ask him to share his experiences with me. I was quite impressed to hear of the church's rapid growth (0 to 200 members in about two years), and their openness to liturgical and musical experimentation. But he recently confessed to me that the church has closed. Why? "We thought we could just do whatever we wanted. We forgot that we needed a structure and we needed a history. We thought it was all about us, and our needs, but it was about the past, and about those who had gone before." When I asked him what happened to its members, he added a bit sheepishly, "Well, a lot of them are now going to the Episcopal Church!"

Manuscript 286 is a symbol for the continuity that Archbishop Parker was looking for. To hold it is to hold the actual book Augustine received from the hands of Pope Gregory, whose hands in turn linked him with those of St. Peter, the first bishop of Rome, the vicar of Christ. Along with his arsenal of historical documents, it helped strengthen that vital link to the past that was so important for Parker and for us. This object of the past holds the key for the future of the church.

— V —

Unity

The visit of Benedict XVI to England in September 2010 was the second by a reigning pope to England since the Reformation, or indeed ever, since none came in the Middle Ages either. In mid-June 2010 I [Dr. Christopher de Hamel] was initially telephoned by Canon Jonathan Goodall, the archbishop of Canterbury's personal chaplain, with what he called "an interesting idea." The plan was, he said, for the pope and the archbishop to preside jointly at an ecumenical service in Westminster Abbey. The reason for choosing the Abbey, rather than, say, the cathedrals of Canterbury (Anglican) or Westminster (Catholic), is because the Abbey is a "royal peculiar," which means it is subject directly to the queen and is independent of the jurisdiction of Canterbury. Therefore the pope and the archbishop would be equal guests of the dean. Westminster Abbey was also once, of course, a Benedictine monastery, and one dedicated to Saint Peter. Would we, Canon Goodall wondered, consider allowing the Gospel Book of Saint Augustine to be carried into the Abbey in the procession and to be jointly reverenced by the pope and the archbishop after the reading of the Gospel text for the day?

The St. Augustine Gospels are both a symbol of the very beginning of the Church in England and it was presumably commissioned by a pope, Saint Gregory, initiator and sponsor of the mission of Augustine.

On the morning of Friday, September 17, I was at the College well before 6. The manuscript had been packed in a bomb-proof case. It was driven in its security van directly to Westminster Abbey and by 8 o'clock we had locked it in the safe below the library in the east range of the cloister, in the care of the Abbey librarian. The whole service was meticulously rehearsed from 11:30 onward. We were all walked through our paces, even the archbishop, who was there (the pope was not), and some last-minute modifications were made to enable appropriate but unobtrusive television coverage.

By midafternoon the whole of Westminster was cordoned off by police. Security was very tight indeed. Reentering the Abbey precincts shortly before 4 o'clock was difficult. We set the manuscript onto its special crimson-silk tray, also prepared for the occasion. We had been asked if the book could be opened at a picture page but this seemed too chancy. Instead we turned it to the Latin words of the Gospel reading for the service, Mark 10:35–45, so that the pope would venerate the actual text just read.

The manuscript and I, however, were taken to the Jerusalem Chamber by the west door (it was the room where Henry IV died). The affable cardinal archbishop of Armagh was already there. One by one, the heads of the various Christian churches of Britain arrived, some already arrayed in underlayers of medieval finery, and others with trim little suitcases, from which mysterious apparel and ornaments were unfolded. Furtively watching them deck themselves, like walking Christmas trees, each after his or her own kind, was an unforgettable pleasure of the day. There were the moderators of the Presbyterian Church and of the Free Churches of England and Wales and of the United Reform Church, chattering to bishops and archbishops; there were the presidents of the Methodist Council and, in striking contrast, of the Council of Oriental Churches in the United Kingdom, with the archbishop of Thyateira and Great Britain; and the Methodist and the Lutheran and the Salvation Army, and many others, gathering and robing. Professor Rackham describes how, sitting in the Abbey, he later counted 200 bishops, like those seen by Don Alhambra in *The Gondoliers,* "Bishops in their shovel hats / were plentiful as tabby cats."

By now the quiet anticipatory rumble of several thousand invited guests in the Abbey was eclipsed by singing and shouting from enormous and motley crowds in the street outside. The cardinal and I watched from the window. There were banners and flags and placards, mostly along the lines of "The Pope is the Antichrist"; next banner: "No, he isn't"; next banner: "Oh, yes, he is"; and so on. A canon switched on a television, so that we could watch the pope's speech in Westminster Hall, which told us too when the papal entourage was about to cross the road toward the Abbey, which was the cue for our strange panoply to move out from the Jerusalem Chamber into positions in the west end of the nave. I was told to stand by a pillar at the grave slab of David Lloyd-George. "Don't you sometimes think, 'What am I doing here?'" I whispered to the polychrome verger beside me, holding the glittering processional Cross of Westminster. He looked puzzled. "No," he said, "not really. This is normal work for us."

The pope's entrance through the west door was heralded by roars of the crowd in the street and the whirring of innumerable cameras, like the sound of ten thousand birds taking flight. After the pope was greeted and robed, we all set off in stately procession down the nave of the Abbey and up through the choir and across the mosaic pavement laid for Henry III in 1268. MS 286 was placed on the high altar, and I bowed (a little) and moved to my seat in the adjacent sedilia. The long procession continued, culminating in the dean, the archbishop of Canterbury, and the pope, with attendant chaplains. Later, after the reading of the Gospel (in English, by the moderator of the Church of

Scotland), my brief task was to bring the manuscript on its
tray to the pope, who bowed and kissed it, and then to turn
to the archbishop, who did the same. My primary worry
was not to slip on the deceptively smooth medieval stone
steps down from the high altar and back again. Tripping
up, which I am capable of doing at the best of times, would
have made spectacular television but would have been bad
for the manuscript. Afterward, during the singing of the
Magnificat, the dean censed the altar, endlessly waving the
smoking thurible back and forth over the manuscript, and
I wondered what I would do if I saw a crumb of smoldering
charcoal landing on the parchment.

In fact, all was well. We cannot now even smell the
incense on the pages. I carried the volume out again, back
to my post on top of Lloyd-George, and I watched the pope
pass by and out into applause in the dusk outside. When the
congregation had dispersed and the streets of Westminster
were reopened, the security van drove into Dean's Yard and
we repacked the manuscript into its place. This time the
Master and Professor Rackham accompanied it home to
Corpus, and by the late evening it was safely back in the
vault in the Parker Library.[1]

Such was the account published by the librarian, Dr.
Christopher de Hamel, in the annual newsletter of Corpus
Christi College following the joint service in Westminster

Abbey on September 17, 2010, at which the heads of both Roman Catholic and Anglican Churches, Pope Benedict XVI and Archbishop Rowan Williams, paid homage to the St. Augustine Gospels as a symbol of the underlying unity between their two churches.

It would seem that the journey of MS 286 has come nearly full circle. It began as a gift of a pope to the first archbishop of Canterbury. Now, more than 1,400 years later, it became a symbol of unity between a pope and the successor of St. Augustine. It is a fitting focal point of a growing awareness of our common spiritual descent as English-speaking Anglicans and Roman Catholics from St. Augustine.

For most of our manuscript's history, that unity did not exist. In the early sixteenth century this Gospel book, for hundreds of years prominently displayed as a tangible and treasured relic of St. Augustine, on the altar of St. Augustine's Abbey in Canterbury, barely escaped the fate of so many other books and ecclesiastical objects destroyed or dispersed at the Dissolution. But thanks to the intervention of Archbishop Matthew Parker, the manuscript found a new home in Cambridge, where it somewhat ironically assumed a new purpose, that of anchoring the new English Church to its Gregorian foundation, before, in Parker's mind, it was distracted by the accretions and corruptions of later popes.

The decision to bring MS 286 into the pope's presence in 2010 was a small but meaningful signal of a detente that has developed between the Church of England and the Roman Catholic Church in recent years. It would be well beyond the scope of this little book to recount the history of the relationship of these two Christian bodies since the English Reformation of the sixteenth century. But the fact that a painful breach is now in the process of being healed is a fact that cannot be denied. Our manuscript played a small but noteworthy role in that process, and serves as a symbol of possible good things to come.

The low point between these two churches occurred in the middle of the 1500s, when the English Reformation caused England to make its final departure from the orbit of Rome. There had been many preludes to this action, and for one to claim that the Church of England exists "because Henry VIII wanted a divorce" is a gross oversimplification. Rumblings of the eventual split are found through the history of the English Church during the medieval period. Indeed, this tension traces its origins as far back as to the conflict between the Celtic Church and the arrival of the Roman missionaries led by St. Augustine.

This tension gained dramatic expression at meetings like the Synod of Whitby (663) and resurfaced throughout the medieval period. Notable examples of England's resentment of papal control were the Statutes of Provisors and Praeminere (1351, 1352) whereby Parliament refused taxation to support the pope's budget. Even Henry VIII's final decision to make a break with Rome, expressed finally in the Act of Succession (1534), was the result of complex diplomatic pressures and occurred only after a long process of threats and negotiations on both sides. Even then, the separation from Rome was hardly a done deal, and continued to be discussed throughout the reigns of Henry, his son Edward VI, and of course Mary, who for a short time brought England back into the Roman orbit. But by the beginning of Elizabeth's reign, thanks to the excesses of her half sister, there was really no hope of reconciliation. Pope Paul V's decision to put a price on the English monarch's head in the bull *Regnans in Excelsis* (1570) transformed the papal curia into a mortal enemy of England. In the eyes of most of its country's citizens, one could no longer be both a loyal Englishman and a Roman Catholic.

The persecution of English Roman Catholics over the succeeding several hundred years is another long, sad tale. On the local level it was expressed in the persistent hounding of Catholics whose religion and priesthood were officially illegal. To hear Mass was in itself a treasonable offense, and these years are marked with the martyrdoms of Roman priests like Edward Campion and others who paid the ultimate price in order to minister to their flocks.

For nearly three hundred years both churches existed in isolation and fear from each other. But thanks to the courageous and controversial actions of a few courageous individuals, relationships were slowly being repaired.

Toward the start of the eighteenth century, the archbishop of Canterbury, William Wake (1716–1737), who had spent much of his earlier career studying in France learning about church affairs there and collecting ancient Greek biblical manuscripts, struck up a long-lasting friendship with

Catholics, especially those "Gallicans" who sought a French Catholic Church largely independent of Rome. His correspondence with one of their leaders, the great patristic scholar Louis Ellies du Pin, had to be kept secret (du Pin was once exiled for his views and his papers seized) and so had little effect.

Efforts to make contact with Rome did not resurface again until the Oxford Movement of the early nineteenth century, when Anglican clergy and Oxford scholars like John Henry Newman, John Keble, and Edward Pusey challenged the assumptions of the established Church of England, which they held to be overly controlled by secular political forces. They pointed out that under English law, members of Parliament, some of whom were not even Christians, were placed in the outrageous position of controlling the Church of England! In their highly controversial *Tracts for the Times*, they called for a return to the ancient apostolic polity of the church. They believed that along with the Eastern Orthodox Church and the Roman Catholic Church, the Anglican Church was one of "three branches" of Orthodox Christianity and that it ought to remain separate from government control.

Although originally a political movement, these Oxford academics were also intrigued by ancient liturgical practices, such as the centrality of the Holy Eucharist, the use of vestments, decorating the altar with candles and flowers, even reviving the monastic orders that had been suppressed at the time of the Reformation. Their ideas were to have a huge impact on the Church of England and even in the

American colonies, although there was also considerable backlash against what many churchmen felt were "Romish" practices or "popery." In England many of these "Anglo-Catholics" went on to follow the example of John Henry Newman, who eventually became a cardinal in the Roman Church. Those who remained in the English Church constituted a "high church" or "ritualist" wing, stressing sacramental life and care for the poorest members of English society (Anglo-Catholic clergy were often refused regular livings and ended up working in the slums).

One of these English "Anglo Catholics," Charles Wood, Second Viscount Halifax (1839–1934), had a lifelong passion for reunification of the church. It was no doubt due to the influence that he exerted in his role as president of the English Church Union that the Lambeth Conference of 1888 addressed the issue of relationship between Rome and Canterbury in a serious manner. The most well-known contribution of this conclave of Anglican bishops from around the world (which has met regularly since 1867 at the invitation of the archbishop of Canterbury to deal with common issues of concerns) was to ratify the work of an earlier American study group which proposed four essential ingredients necessary for union with other churches.

This Lambeth Quadrilateral, as it came to be called, is familiar to modern Episcopalians who can peruse it in the Historical Documents section at the back of the Book of Common Prayer. Briefly stated, it insists upon:

1. Scripture as the ultimate standard of faith
2. The ancient creeds of the church as the "sufficient state-ment" of the faith
3. The two sacraments of Baptism and Eucharist minis-tered unfailingly
4. The historic episcopate, "locally adapted in the meth-ods of its administration"[2]

This last point has proved a sticking point in subsequent ecumenical conversations with Reformed churches, but in its original form, it went far in clearing a path for Anglicans and Roman Catholics to recognize each other's hierarchical structure, if not their theological agreement. For example, would it be possible under this blueprint for Anglicans to accept the spiritual primacy of the bishop of Rome?

Immediately following the 1888 Lambeth Conference, Lord Halifax began serious conversations with his friend, the Belgian Abbe Ferdinand Portal. Portal recognized that if any real union were to take place, it would come about not simply as "reabsorption" of the Anglicans by Rome but through a mutual recognition of their common ministry. Thus it was a necessary first step that Rome accept the valid-ity of Anglican orders and recognize that Anglican bishops, priests, and deacons were ordained to the same sacred call-ing as their Roman Catholic counterparts. Before weightier issues of governance and doctrine could be discussed, each side had to recognize themselves as equals.

This, however, was simply too much for the Vatican to swallow. After study and deliberation, the bull *Apostolicae Curae* was released and endorsed by Pope Leo XIII in 1896. Its contents were a severe blow to the work of Lord Halifax and Abbe Portal, for its language was absolute and uncompromising, Anglican orders were "absolutely null and utterly void." Further, this understanding of the Holy See brooked no discussion, for the decision was "always valid and in force and shall be inviolably observed." It should be noted however that many subsequent Catholic theologians have in fact taken issue with this decision. Officially the "hardline" has prevailed, as Benedict XVI himself confirmed in his bull *Anglicanorum coetibus* (2009), which created Anglican "ordinariates" in which Anglicans could reenter the Catholic Church while maintaining their own Anglican liturgical vocabulary and practices, in effect becoming another uniate church (like the Eastern Catholic Church) clearly subject to Rome. At the time of this writing, there are some hopeful indications that Pope Francis I may distance himself from this rigid understanding.

With the publication of *Apostolicae Curae,* the diplomatic relationship between the two churches seemed to be at an unprecedented low, and yet the quest for unity was to gain energy from a new source outside both churches: the worldwide ecumenical movement. Protestant churches were the driving force behind the meeting in Edinburgh in 1910 of the World Missionary Conference. About 1,200 delegates from many churches around the world attended, and included such noteworthy figures as the American politician William Jennings Bryan. They had been brought together by a concern over "modernism" resulting from advances in science—particularly the teaching of evolution—and historical-critical approaches to the Bible. How was the church to react to these twentieth-century challenges? Being united against a common threat also led to a greater understanding of their divisions. The ecumenical movement had been launched and was to lead eventually to the creation of the World Council of Churches in 1948.

What is ecumenism? The word comes from the Greek world for "whole household" (*oikomenos*) and implies that there is an underlying unity in Christ that has the power to bring all churches together. This does not mean the creation of some vast "super church" as opponents of the World Council of Churches often claim, but rather a mutual sense of respect and cooperation between Christian bodies. In the words of a classic definition, ecumenism is "a movement that aims at the recovery in thought, action, and in organization, of the true unity between the church's mission to the world and the church's obligation to be one."[3]

Inspired by the work of the ecumenical movement, the bishops of the Anglican Communion were to revisit the topic in the Lambeth gathering of 1920. They optimistically proclaimed:

> The times call us to a new outlook and new measures.
> The Faith cannot be adequately apprehended and the

battle of the Kingdom be worthily fought while the body is divided. . . . The time has come, we believe, for all the separated groups of Christians to agree in forgetting the things that are behind and reaching towards the goal of a reunited Catholic Church.[4]

Making this vision a reality was delegated to the Malines Conference of 1921. The talks were secret and informal because of the fear of reaction on both sides. Catholic representatives went into the meeting still under the impression that any future close relationship with Anglicans meant their reabsorption of that church. Anglicans, on the other hand, were looking at a variety of options. Although there was obviously no official policy to come out of the meeting, the results, as Pope Paul VI was to say many years later, were "epoch-making." This new outlook was summed up by Belgian Cardinal Mercier: Speaking for the conference, he said that the "Anglican Church was to be united with Rome, not absorbed." This approach laid the groundwork for all future discussions. It formed the backdrop for two important future papal bulls: *Unitatis redintegratio,* which came from the discussions of the Second Vatican Council (1962) and *Ut unum sint* (1995). Both documents make it clear that unity between the Roman Church and other Christian bodies is the inevitable result of the work of the Holy Spirit.

The theoretical foundation for the unity of the church has now been clearly established. It has played itself out in three principle ways: (1) high-level theological discussion,

(2) liturgical study and sharing, and (3) local grassroots cooperation in addressing social justice issues.

Since the days of Vatican II, there have been several generations of high-level ecumenical dialogue dealing with different topics under the umbrella of the Anglican–Roman Catholic International Commission (ARCIC) founded by Archbishop of Canterbury Michael Ramsey and Pope Paul VI in 1967. The first phase of its work, completed in 1981, dealt with the topics of the Eucharist, ministry, and authority. The second phase focused on a wider range of issues and concluded with the publication of *Mary: Grace and Hope in Christ* in 2005. ARCIC III has had three meetings, most recently in 2013 in Rio de Janeiro, and has dealt with the ethical teachings of the church. However this latest phase has been hampered by actions in the Anglican Communion that the Roman Catholic side finds unacceptable, such as the ordination of women to the priesthood and the ordination by the Episcopal Church of openly gay and lesbian bishops, beginning with the consecration of Gene Robinson in 2003. It remains to be seen how these obstacles might be overcome.

In spite of these official tensions, there remain good relationships between both the pope and the archbishop of Canterbury. There have been papal visits to England by John Paul II in 1982 and Benedict XVI in 2010 (in both of which the St. Augustine Gospels was involved). In addition, the archbishops of Canterbury have had several private audiences with the pope, beginning with Geoffrey Fisher in 1960 and continuing as recently as 2013, when Justin Welby assumed office as the 105th archbishop of Canterbury and met with Pope Francis. The Anglican Centre in Rome, founded by Archbishop Michael Ramsey and Pope Paul VI in 1966, has continued in an informal way the dialogue envisioned by the Second Vatican Council.

A more grassroots movement toward unity has come not from hierarchical pronouncements but from shared experiences of worship. Since the nineteenth century, the liturgical renewal movement has deeply affected the ways that ordinary Anglican and Roman Catholics worship on Sunday morning and has brought the two churches ever closer together. Wikipedia concisely describes this movement:

> First, it was an attempt to rediscover the worship practices of the Middle Ages, which in the 19th century was held to be the ideal form of worship and expression of faith. Second, it developed as scholarship to study and analyze the history of worship. Third, it broadened into an examination of the nature of worship as an organic human activity. Fourth, it attempted to renew worship in order that it could be more expressive for worshippers and as an instrument of teaching and mission. Fifth, it has been a movement attempting to bring about reconciliation among the churches on both sides of the Protestant Reformation.[5]

The Roman Catholic origins of these efforts go back to the 1830s when the Benedictine community at Solesmes Abbey in France began a critical study of Gregorian Chant and other ancient liturgical practices. Soon after, patristic studies received a major boost through the efforts of Abbe Jacques-Paul Migne, who compiled vast collections of the early fathers of the church. In 1875, the early Christian instruction manual of Eucharistic practice called the *Didache* (or Teaching) was discovered. Having this window into the worship life of the early church had a huge impact on subsequent scholars. Such critical study received the papal seal of approval by Pope Pius X, whose pontificate in the early twentieth century encouraged such practices as use of the vernacular in the Mass and frequent communion by the laity. Many of these changes were later endorsed and expanded by the Second Vatican Council.

On the Anglican side, the interest shown by the members of the Oxford Movement and their desire for ancient catholic worship, including the reinstatement of vestments, had its effect on subsequent reforms of the Prayer Book liturgy. A major contributor to liturgical scholarship was the English monk Dom Gregory Dix, whose book *The Shape of the Liturgy* is required reading for seminarians to this day. Dom Dix was in direct contact with studies taking place among continental Roman Catholic scholars. His work was largely responsible for returning the Eucharist to its central place in Anglican and Episcopal worship.

We can see all of these currents reflected in the ordinary worship lives of today's Episcopalians. Indeed it is almost impossible for us in the church now to recall a time when Morning Prayer was the principal Sunday service, bishops made visitations in a black rochet and chimere, and infants were baptized privately in a corner at the rear of the church on a Saturday afternoon. Ancient practices that would have been labeled by our Anglican grandparents as "popish" are now a common part of everyday liturgical life. Included on this list would be such practices as use of chant, incense, icons, and walking the labyrinth. Such expressions of the faith are, as we have seen, deeply attractive to those seeking to connect to their spiritual roots. For example, the community of Taizé in France, operated by monks from both Catholic and Protestant backgrounds, provides an immersion experience for thousands of pilgrims, many of them young, each year. Their chant-like music has found its way into the common usage of many congregations.

Anglicans and Catholics are worshipping in increasingly common ways, borrowing and adapting the best parts of each other's traditions. This process is a two-way street. Anglicans may look to Rome to guide them in an increasingly rich liturgical life, but Catholics have also begun to place a greater emphasis on biblical preaching and the inclusion of laity in worship, historically the strong suit of Anglicans and other Protestant groups. Some new expressions of Christianity have even taken this borrowing to a higher level, as self-defined "emergent churches" feel free to use the most meaningful expressions of theology and worship from both Protestant and Catholic sources.

Official dogmatic and liturgical expressions of unity between Roman Catholics and Anglicans (as well as other churches) may receive more media attention, but no less powerful are the efforts made by congregations from both bodies to address common social and political justice issues. In contrast to "top-down" statements of common belief and practice coming from the hierarchy, congregations are increasingly working together on a host of issues affecting them locally. We might term this "grassroots" or "bottom-up" ecumenism, and it has the potential of accomplishing far more than official pronouncements. There has been wide agreement on a host of topics such as education, healthcare, and immigration, though members of both churches may find themselves on opposite sides of the fence when it comes to such issues as abortion, birth control, and human sexuality. Yet it appears that even those topics might receive a new consideration under the pontificate of Francis I.

A small example of this new climate is the cooperative spirit and support this author has experienced working with episcopal colleagues from the Roman Catholic, Lutheran, and Methodist churches as we have taken a role in addressing the immigration crisis on Arizona's border with Mexico. Together, we have made public witnesses over the inhumane treatment of undocumented people. We often found ourselves on the same speaking platform, at meetings with political leaders, or marching in demonstrations. We even wrote a book together! Entitled *Bishops on the Border,* it documented how our experience working together has changed our lives and souls.

Such work together brings us back full circle to the quest for unity. Unity in theology, worship, and liturgy finds its ultimate expression in unity of mission, that same impulse to share the Good News of Jesus that drove Pope Gregory to commission St. Augustine to be an apostle for the English people. For the mission of the church is the same as the Great Commission that Jesus gave to his disciples (and hence us) at the end of his earthly ministry, to "go therefore unto all nations, teaching them all that I have told you, and baptizing them in the name of the Father, the Son, and of the Holy Spirit." Such is the Good News that all Christians must share. Such is the mission that ultimately binds us together.

Our manuscript of course is vastly remote in time from the issues that keep us apart as churches today. When it was created, there was only one Christendom, and that was centered in Rome. The issues that cause controversy today were unknown and unimaginable at the time of Pope Gregory's headship. Perhaps this is one reason why his gift to St. Augustine has become today such a moving symbol of the possibility for unity between Roman Catholics and Anglicans. The earliest Gospel book in England came from Rome, a gift from the bishop of Rome, and it is the same Gospel book upon which the archbishop of

Canterbury takes his oath of office. Now with the visit of Pope Benedict, it has been handled and venerated by the successor to St. Peter.

It is a powerful reminder that the gospel of Jesus Christ is the same yesterday today and tomorrow (Heb. 13:8) and that Jesus's prayer for the church remains—"that we all may be one."

Postscript

Manuscript 286 has traveled only about a hundred miles in the more than 1,400 years since it arrived in England. During its long residences at St. Augustine's Abbey in Canterbury and the Parker Library in Cambridge, it has been seen and read by a relative handful of people, yet its story has influenced history in ways that vastly exceed its humble status. It provided inspiration for a group of monks who were to re-Christianize England in the sixth century. It was an object of veneration for English churchmen of the medieval period. It was a powerful link to the past for one of the principal architects of the English Reformation. It serves as a powerful liturgical reminder to modern English primates of their link with St. Augustine and provides a background for discussions between Christendom's two largest bodies, the Anglican Communion and the Roman Catholic Church. It can truly be said to be one of the most important medieval manuscripts in existence, on par with the Book of Kells, the Domesday Book, and the Magna Carta.

Without question, the St. Augustine Gospels has made a profound contribution to our study of the past, especially that of the early days of the English Church, but it also points the way to a Christianity of the future. The fact that it was created as a tool for mission, that it used the best technology of its day, that it helped stabilize the English Church in a revolutionary period of change, and that it symbolizes the common dream for unity among many Christians means that it incarnates the four ingredients needed if the church is to flourish in an increasingly materialistic and secular age. Those key ingredients, we have suggested, are an emphasis on sharing the gospel with all people, a willingness to embrace media, a reaffirmation of the core values of the apostolic church, and a search for common ground among all branches of Christianity. In short, they are the ingredients of mission, communication, continuity, and unity.

It is extremely gratifying to see that these themes, embodied in ancient parchment and ink, are more than just a recipe for the future but are actually being lived out in congregations today. To share just a few images of each:

MISSION

Although this word is used, misused, and overused, it is now part of nearly every conversation among leaders of the church. In the Episcopal Church in the United States, the legal corporate name of which is "The Domestic and Foreign Missionary Society of the United States of America," it has recently been suggested that we actually begin to publicly describe ourselves as "The Missionary Society," rather than as a "church." This reflects a growing awareness that for the church to grow, its efforts must be focused on those who are outside of its institutional walls, especially those groups who are alienated from "organized religion," such as youth and immigrants.

The prophetic words of the former archbishop of Canterbury Michael Ramsey are being taken increasingly seriously: "The Church that lives for itself, dies by itself,"[1] which means that the energy and resources of the church must be directed toward those who are not its members! This has been, and continues to be, a hard lesson for the religious establishment to learn, but there are some encouraging signs. For the first time in its history, at its last General Convention the Episcopal Church directed several million dollars of its budget toward the planting of new churches, all in "missional areas." The Volunteers in Mission Program and the Episcopal Service Corps, modeled after the Peace Corps, have attracted a growing number of young people desiring to live in service in poor areas of this country and overseas. An increasing number of local congregations are reaching out in effective ways (in time and not just money) to local agencies that work together to better the community. As former Presiding Bishop Katharine Jefferts Schori rightly points out, "Mission is the heartbeat of the church."[2]

Communication

Those of us past middle age are often bemused that we can remember a day when there were no personal computers or cell phones. St. Augustine could remember a day when there were no pictures in manuscripts. As we have pointed out, MS 286 is the earliest book in existence to contain a picture of Jesus at the Last Supper. This was nothing short of revolutionary in its time, for the Anglo-Saxon people had no visual art of any kind. The medieval church wasted no time employing the visual arts to the purpose of teaching and evangelism. This was vitally necessary in a time when most of the population could neither read nor write. But they could look at pictures, which they increasing found in books, murals, tapestries, and most gloriously, in stained-glass windows.

In our own time, after some initial reluctance, congregations are beginning to put the new digital technologies to work. There are few local churches today that don't have their own website or Facebook page, and woe to the bishop who fails to blog or tweet! Social media holds the promise of relationship building on a scale unimagined just a generation ago. Indeed, we clergy who use technology are coming to have a larger audience on the web and in social media than we do of folks who sit in the pews on a Sunday morning! Surely this new connectivity holds enormous promise for the communication of the gospel to all people.

Continuity

Pastor and theologian Dan Kimball puts it succinctly: "How ironic that returning to a raw and ancient form of worship is now seen as new and even cutting edge. We are simply going back to a vintage form of worship that has been around for as long as the church has been in existence."[3] What promise this statement holds for those of us who come from churches who pride ourselves on offering "traditional" worship! We are increasingly valuing those forms of expression that have tremendous appeal to Gen X and Gen Y worshipers: labyrinths, icons, meditation, fasting, incense, and chant.

In rediscovering our continuity with the faith and practice of the early church, we are following the lead of Archbishop Matthew Parker who sought to anchor a newly reformed English Church to its ancient foundations. Manuscript 286 was an important part of the library he assembled for that purpose. The fact that his successors have used it as the Gospel book on which to swear their oath of office makes this dramatically clear: The twenty-first-century Church of England is insolubly bound with the sixth-century church of Rome.

Unity

An essential unity between the Anglican and Roman Catholic churches was confirmed when Pope Benedict XVI visited England in 2010. In their mutual veneration of the St. Augustine Gospels, the pope and Archbishop Rowan Williams made it clear for the world to see that Roman Catholics and Anglicans, despite their differences, share a fundamental belief, a common history, and joint hope for the future.

Manuscript 286, this most ancient of books, has brought us full circle to a time of new hopefulness. It was written for men who aspired to bring the Good News to a strange and foreign land. It now serves a church that struggles to make that message available to the equally strange and even hostile culture of the twenty-first century. It symbolizes the hope that by honoring the gospel and applying its message in new ways, we can have a church that moves beyond itself in common purpose and in common fellowship, one in which even the pope and the archbishop of Canterbury can ask each other's blessing.

The St. Augustine Gospels may be the oldest book in England, but it is after all a Bible, and that ancient Word, we can be sure, will endure forever.

Notes

CHAPTER 1

1. Bede, *The Ecclesiastical History of the English People,* bk. 2., ch. 1 (London: George Bell and Sons, 1907), 82.
2. Reported by John the Deacon in the ninth century. Jeffrey Richards, *Consul of God: The Life and Times of Gregory the Great* (London: Routledge & Kegan Paul, 1980), 44.
3. F. L. Cross, ed. *Institutes of the Christian Religion* (1515), quoted in "Gregory the Great," Wikipedia.
4. Bede, 4.
5. Bede, 161.
6. Bede, 43.
7. Bede. 46.
8. Ian Wood, "The Mission of Augustine to the English," *Speculum* 69 (Jan 1994), 15.
9. Bede, 67.
10. Bede, 87.
11. *Mission-Shaped Church* (London: Church House Publishing, 2004).

12. David J. Bosch, *Transforming Mission* (Maryknoll, NY: Orbis, 1991), 389–391.

13. Rowan Williams, Archbishop's retreat address, pt. 1 (July 17, 2008).

14. The Book of Common Prayer (hereafter BCP) (New York: Church Publishing, 1979), 838.

15. BCP, 257.

16. BCP, 247.

17. BCP, 257.

18. BCP, 855.

19. BCP, 257.

20. http://www.episcopalchurch.org/library/article/mission-all-all.

21. See David Kinnaman and Gabe Lyons, *Unchristian: What a New Generation Really Thinks about Christianity . . . and Why It Matters* (Grand Rapids, MI: Baker Books, 2007).

22. *Mission-Shaped Church*, xi.

23. Bosch, *Transforming Mission*, 16.

24. Bosch, *Transforming Mission*, 8

25. Katharine Jefferts Schori, Sermon to General Convention, July 8, 2009.

CHAPTER 2

1. For more information on the MS itself, see the upcoming study by Christopher de Hamel, *Interviews with Manuscripts*, (London: Allen Lane, 2016).

2. Mildred Budny, *Insular, Anglo-Sacon and Early Anglo-Norman Manuscript Art at Corpus Christi College* (Kalamazoo, MI: Medieval Institute Publications, 1997), 3.

3. Budny, 9.

4. Bede, 65.

5. Folio 17r-v.

6. Budny, 11.

7. John Bale, Corrrespondence in Cambridge University Library, MS Add. 7489, f. 17.

CHAPTER 3

1. Michelle Brown, *Manuscripts from the Anglo-Saxon Age* (London: The British Library, 2007), 10.

2. Christopher de Hamel, *A History of Illuminated Manuscripts* (Boston: David R. Godine, 1986), 11.

3. *Wikipedia,* s.v. digital revolution, last modified October 3, 2015, https://en.wikipedia.org/wiki/Digital_Revolution.

4. In the interest of full disclosure, I should note that Drescher makes reference in her first book to my use of social media in a diocesan setting.

5. Elizabeth Drescher, *Tweet If You [Heart] Jesus: Practicing Church in the Digital Reformation* (New York: Morehouse Publishing, 2011), xii.

6. Drescher, *Tweet,* 25.

7. March 19, 2012.

8. Ibid.

9. Eugene Sutton, *USA Today,* June 21, 2010.

10. Christopher Heine, "70% Of Marketers Will Spend More on Social Media Ads This Year." *Adweek,* Jan. 12, 2015.

11. Elizabeth Drescher, "Social Media Rebooting Religion," SFGate (June 5, 2011), http://www.sfgate.com/opinion/article/Social -media-rebooting-religion-2368715.php.

12. David Roach, "Research: Churches Divided on Web Use," Lifeway (Jan. 21, 2011), http://www.lifeway.com/ArticleView?storeId =10054&catalogId=10001&langId=-1&article=LifeWay-Research -Churches-divided-web-use.

13. Interview with Bishop Doyle, Feb. 16, 2013.

14. Drescher, *Tweet,* 137ff.

15. Drescher, *Tweet,* 157ff.

16. Read more at http://www.brainyquote.com/quotes/authors/d/don_tapscott.html.

Chapter 4

1. "Matthew Parker," *Wikipedia.* See also V. J. K. Brook, *A Life of Archbishop Parker* (Oxford: Clarendon Press, 1962), 15.
2. Lacey Baldwin Smith, *The Elizabethan World* (Boston: Houghton Mifflin, 1967), 73.
3. The Bishop's Bible, 1568.
4. For full text of the Act, see http://history.hanover.edu/texts/engref/er80.html.
5. Brook, 183–186.
6. Parker, *De Antiquitate Ecclesiae* (1572). 45.
7. John Strype, *Annals of the Reformation and Establishment of Religion* (London: n.p., 1824), 2:520.
8. S.W. Kershaw, "Archbishop Parker, Collector and Author," *The Library* n.s.I (1900), 381.
9. Ibid, 382.
10. See http://complinechoir.org.
11. Diana Butler Bass, *The Practicing Congregation: Imagining a New Old Church* (Herndon, VA: Alban Institute, 2004), 3.
12. Bass, *The Practicing Congregation,* 50.
13. Eddie Gibbs and Ryan Bolger, *Emerging Churches: Creating Christian Community in Postmodern Cultures* (Grand Rapids, MI: Baker Academic, 2005), 44–45.
14. Tony Jones, *The New Christians: Dispatches from the Emergent Frontier* (San Francisco: Jossey-Bass, 2008), 53.
15. Phyllis Tickle, *The Great Emergence: How Christianity Is Changing and Why* (Grand Rapids, MI: Baker Books, 2008), 16.
16. "Emerging Church," *Wikipedia* (accessed August 14, 2015).
17. D. A. Carson, *Becoming Conversant with the Emerging Church: Understanding a Movement and Its Implications* (Grand Rapids, MI: Zondervan, 2005), 27.

18. Dan Kimball, *The Emerging Church: Vintage Christianity for New Generations* (Grand Rapids, MI: Zondervan, 2003).

19. Robert Webber, *Evangelicals on the Canterbury Trail: Why Evangelicals Are Attracted to the Liturgical Church* (Waco, TX: Word Books, 1985).

20. Joan Huyser-Honig and Darrell Harris, "Robert Webber's Legacy: Ancient Future Faith and Worship," Calvin Institute of Christian Worship, http://worship.calvin.edu/resources/resource-library/robert-e-webber-s-legacy-ancient-future-faith-and-worship/.

21. Ibid.

22. Ibid.

23. Ibid.

24. Robert Webber, "A Call to an Ancient Evangelical Future," *Christianity Today* (Sept. 1, 2006). http://www.christianitytoday.com/ct/2006/september/11.57.html.

25. Engaging God's Mission in the 21st Century: Final Report of the Task Force for Reimagining the Episcopal Church (TREC), September 4, 2014, 4. Available at https://extranet.general convention.org/staff/files/download/12219.pdf.

CHAPTER 5

1. Dr. Christopher de Hamel, annual newsletter of Corpus Christi College.

2. BCP, 877.

3. World Council of Churches, statement of purpose at http://www.oikoumene.org/.

4. Lambeth Conference, 1920, quoted in Mary Reath, *Rome and Canterbury: The Elusive Search for Unity* (Lanham, MD: Rowman and Littlefield, 2007).

5. *Wikipedia*, s.v. liturgical movement, last modified June 9, 2015, https://en.wikipedia.org/wiki/Liturgical_Movement.

Postscript

1. Speech to Anglican leaders, 1963, quoted in http://www.anglican journal.com/articles/-a-church-which-lives-to-itself-will-die-by -itself.

2. Katharine Jefferts Schori, *The Heartbeat of God: Finding the Sacred in the Middle of Everything* (Woodstock, VT: SkyLight Paths, 2011).

3. Dan Kimball, *The Emerging Church: Vintage Christianity for New Generations* (Grand Rapids, MI: Zondervan, 2003),